Kaplan Publishing are constantly finding new ways to support students looking for exam success and our online resources really do add an extra dimension to your studies.

This book comes with free MyKaplan online resources so that you can study anytime, anywhere. **This free online resource is not sold separately and is included in the price of the book.**

Having purchased this book, you have access to the following online study materials:

| CONTENT | AAT | |
| --- | --- | --- |
| | Text | Kit |
| Electronic version of the book | ✓ | ✓ |
| Knowledge Check tests with instant answers | ✓ | |
| Mock assessments online | ✓ | ✓ |
| Material updates | ✓ | ✓ |

CW01496436

## How to access your online resources

**Received this book as part of your Kaplan course?**
If you have a MyKaplan account, your full online resources will be added automatically, in line with the information in your course confirmation email. If you've not used MyKaplan before, you'll be sent an activation email once your resources are ready.

**Bought your book from Kaplan?**
We'll automatically add your online resources to your MyKaplan account. If you've not used MyKaplan before, you'll be sent an activation email.

**Bought your book from elsewhere?**
Go to **www.mykaplan.co.uk/add-online-resources**
Enter the ISBN number found on the title page and back cover of this book.
Add the unique pass key number contained in the scratch panel below.
You may be required to enter additional information during this process to set up or confirm your account details.

This code can only be used once for the registration of this book online. This registration and your online content will expire when the examinations covered by this book have taken place. Please allow one hour from the time you submit your book details for us to process your request.

Please scratch the film to access your unique code.

Please be aware that this code is case-sensitive and you will need to include the dashes within the passcode, but not when entering the ISBN.

PUBLISHING

**British Library Cataloguing-in-Publication Data**

A catalogue record for this book is available from the British Library.

Published by:

Kaplan Publishing UK

Unit 2 The Business Centre

Molly Millar's Lane

Wokingham

Berkshire

RG41 2QZ

ISBN: 978-1-83996-892-1

© Kaplan Financial Limited, 2024

Printed and bound in Great Britain

**Acknowledgements**

We are grateful to HM Revenue and Customs for the provision of tax forms, which are Crown Copyright and are reproduced here with kind permission from the Office of Public Sector Information.

# AAT

# Q2022

# Tax Processes for Businesses
# Finance Act 2024

# EXAM KIT

This Exam Kit supports study for the following AAT qualifications:

AAT Level 3 Diploma in Accounting

AAT Level 3 Certificate in Bookkeeping

AAT Diploma in Accounting at SCQF Level 7

# CONTENTS

**Features in this exam kit**

In addition to providing a wide ranging bank of real assessment style questions, we have also included in this kit:

- unit specific information and advice on assessment technique
- our recommended approach to make your revision for this particular unit as effective as possible.

You will find a wealth of other resources to help you with your studies on the Kaplan and AAT websites:

www.mykaplan.co.uk

www.aat.org.uk/

Quality and accuracy are of the utmost importance to us so if you spot an error in any of our products, please send an email to mykaplanreporting@kaplan.com with full details, or follow the link to the feedback form in MyKaplan.

Our Quality Coordinator will work with our technical team to verify the error and take action to ensure it is corrected in future editions.

# INDEX TO QUESTIONS AND ANSWERS

KAPLAN PUBLISHING

## ANSWER ENHANCEMENTS

We have added the following enhancements to the answers in this exam kit:

**Key answer tips**

Some answers include key answer tips to help your understanding of each question.

*Tutorial note*

Some answers include tutorial notes to explain some of the technical points in more detail.

# ASSESSMENT TECHNIQUE

- **Do not skip any of the** material in the syllabus.

- **Read each question** very carefully.

- In calculative style questions if you are provided with rounding rules (e.g. round to the nearest pence) you **must** follow these to gain credit.

- **Double-check your answer** before committing yourself to it.

- Answer **every** question – if you do not know an answer to a multiple choice question or true/false question, you don't lose anything by guessing. Think carefully before you **guess**.

- If you are answering a multiple-choice question, **eliminate first those answers that you know are wrong**. Then choose the most appropriate answer from those that are left.

- **Don't panic** if you realise you've answered a question incorrectly. Getting one question wrong will not mean the difference between passing and failing.

## COMPUTER-BASED ASSESSMENTS – TIPS

- Do not attempt a CBA until you have **completed all study material** relating to it.

- On the AAT website, there is a CBA demonstration. It is **ESSENTIAL** that you attempt this before your real CBA. You will become familiar with how to move around the CBA screens and the way that questions are formatted, increasing your confidence and speed in the actual assessment.

- Be sure you understand how to use the **software** before you start the assessment. If in doubt, ask the assessment centre staff to explain it to you.

- Questions are **displayed on the screen** and answers are entered using keyboard and mouse. At the end of the assessment, you are given a certificate showing the result you have achieved unless some manual marking is required for the assessment.

- In addition to the traditional multiple-choice question type, CBAs will also contain **other types of questions**, such as number entry questions, drag and drop, true/false, pick lists or drop down menus or hybrids of these.

- In some CBAs you may have to type in complete computations or written answers.

- You need to be sure you **know how to answer questions** of this type before you sit the real assessment, through practice.

# UNIT SPECIFIC INFORMATION

## THE ASSESSMENT

### FORMAT OF THE ASSESSMENT

Learners will be assessed by computer-based assessment. All questions in the TPFB assessment are computer marked.

In any one assessment, learners may not be assessed on all content, or on the full depth or breadth of a piece of content. The content assessed may change over time to ensure validity of assessment, but all assessment criteria will be tested over time.

The learning outcomes for this unit are as follows:

| | Learning outcome | Weighting |
|---|---|---|
| 1 | Understand legislation requirements relating to VAT | 25% |
| 2 | Calculate VAT | 30% |
| 3 | Review and verify VAT returns | 20% |
| 4 | Understand principles of payroll | 15% |
| 5 | Report information within the organisation | 10% |
| | Total | 100% |

### Time allowed

1 hour 30 minutes

### PASS MARK

The pass mark for all AAT CBAs is 70%.

 **Always keep your eye on the clock and make sure you attempt all questions!**

## DETAILED SYLLABUS

The detailed syllabus and study guide written by the AAT can be found at:

www.aat.org.uk

# REFERENCE MATERIAL IN YOUR ASSESSMENT

In the assessment, you will be provided with comprehensive reference material.

You can access this by clicking on the 'references' link at the right hand side of the screen then by selecting the appropriate heading for the information you wish to view.

The reference material is available on the AAT website and is included at the end of this section of the exam kit. You should refer to it when you work through questions. It is important to know what is in the material and what is not!

Throughout the answers in the kit, we have referred to this material as follows:

**Key answer tips**

Information about this topic is included in the reference material provided in the real assessment, so you do not need to learn it.

However, you need to be familiar with its location and content – why not look at it now?

# KAPLAN'S RECOMMENDED REVISION APPROACH

## QUESTION PRACTICE IS THE KEY TO SUCCESS

Success in professional examinations relies upon you acquiring a firm grasp of the required knowledge at the tuition phase. In order to be able to do the questions, knowledge is essential.

However, the difference between success and failure often hinges on your assessment technique on the day and making the most of the revision phase of your studies.

The **Kaplan study text** is the starting point, designed to provide the underpinning knowledge to tackle all questions. However, in the revision phase, poring over textbooks is not the answer.

**Kaplan pocket notes** are designed to help you quickly revise a topic area; however, you then need to practise questions. There is a need to progress to assessment style questions as soon as possible, and to tie your assessment technique and technical knowledge together.

**The importance of question practice cannot be over-emphasised.**

The recommended approach below is designed by expert tutors in the field, in conjunction with their knowledge of the chief examiner and the sample assessment.

**You need to practise as many questions as possible in the time you have left.**

## OUR AIM

Our aim is to get you to the stage where you can attempt assessment questions confidently, to time, in a closed book environment, with no supplementary help (i.e. to simulate the real assessment experience).

Practising your assessment technique is also vitally important for you to assess your progress and identify areas of weakness that may need more attention in the final run up to the real assessment.

In order to achieve this we recognise that initially you may feel the need to practise some questions with open book help.

**Good assessment technique is vital.**

# THE KAPLAN REVISION PLAN

## STAGE 1:    ASSESS AREAS OF STRENGTH AND WEAKNESS

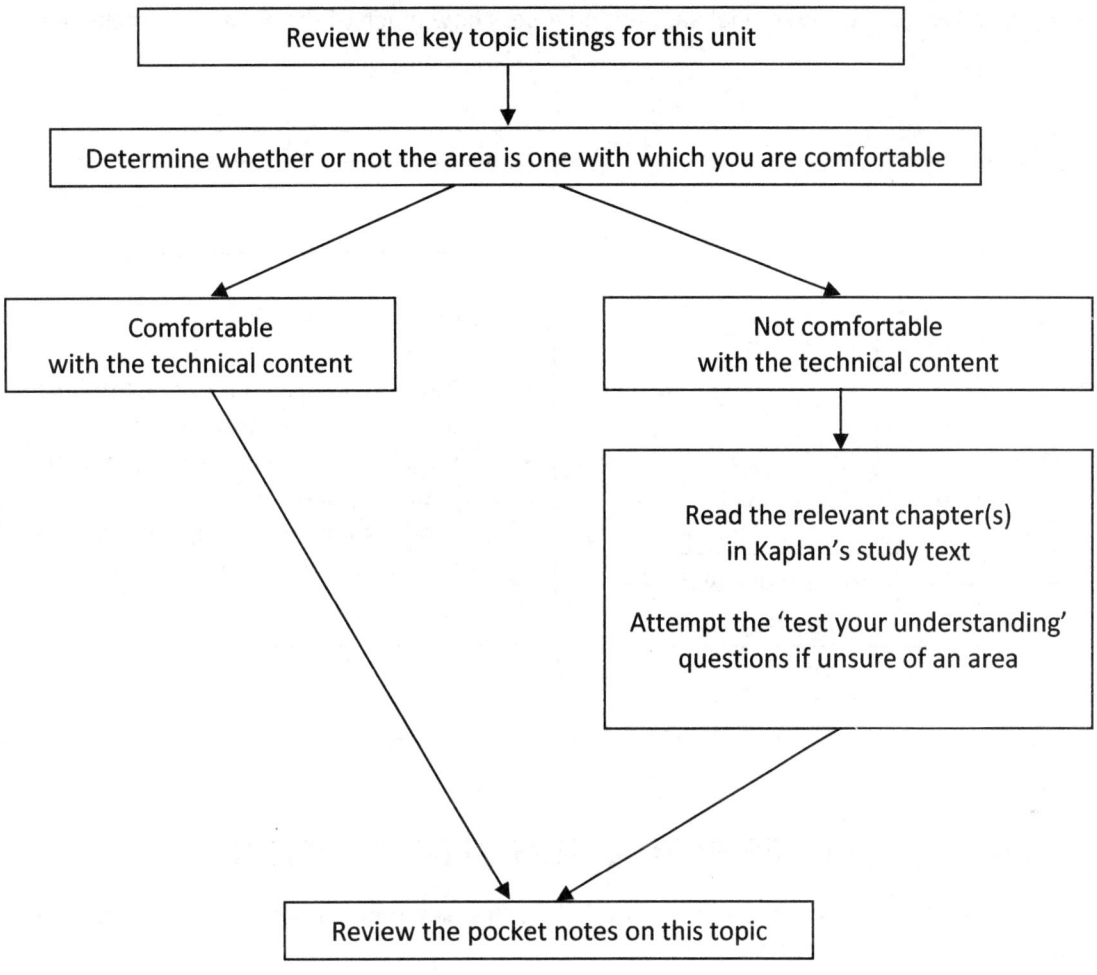

## STAGE 2: PRACTICE QUESTIONS

Follow the order of revision of topics as presented in this kit and attempt the questions in the order suggested.

Try to avoid referring to study texts and your notes and the model answer until you have completed your attempt.

Review your attempt with the model answer and assess how much of the answer you achieved.

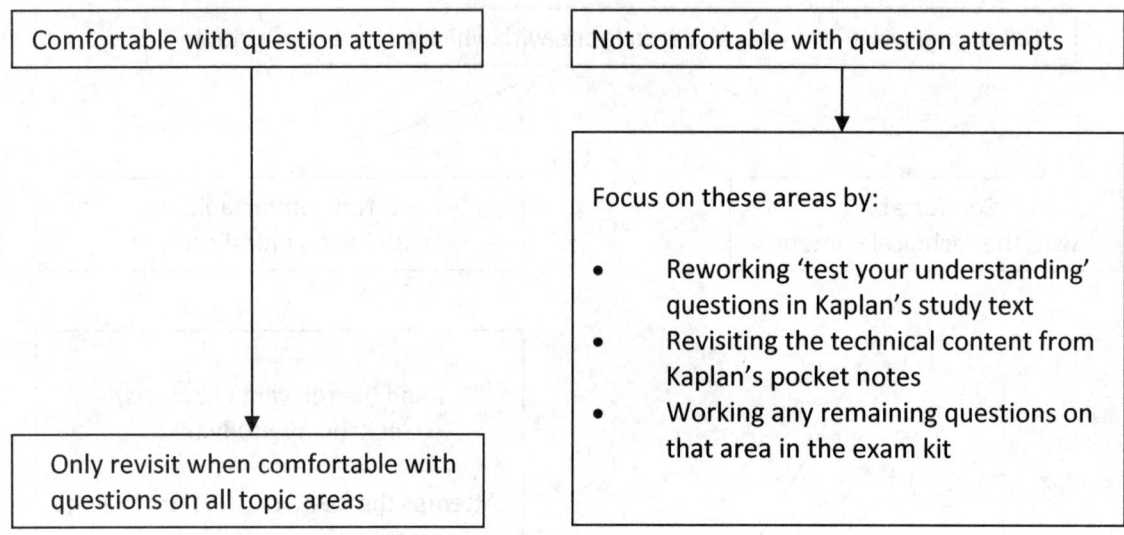

## STAGE 3: FINAL PRE-REAL ASSESSMENT REVISION

We recommend that you **attempt at least one full mock assessment** containing a set of previously unseen real assessment standard questions.

Attempt the mock CBA online in timed, closed book conditions to simulate the real assessment experience.

You will find a mock CBA for this unit at www.mykaplan.co.uk

# REFERENCE INFORMATION

The following information will be provided in the real assessment via a series of clickable links. This information is provided here for ease of reference as you progress through this workbook. You should not take a printed copy into the exam

# Level 3 Tax Processes for Businesses (TPFB) reference material

**Finance Act 2024** – for assessments from 27 January 2025

aat.org.uk

# Reference material for AAT assessment of Tax Processes for Businesses

## Introduction

This document comprises data that you may need to consult during your Tax Processes for Businesses computer-based assessment.

The material can be consulted during the practice and live assessments by using the reference materials section at each task position. It's made available here so you can familiarise yourself with the content before the assessment.

Do not take a print of this document into the exam room with you*.

This document may be changed to reflect periodical updates in the computer-based assessment, so please check you have the most recent version while studying. This version is based on **Finance Act 2024** and is for use in **AAT Q2022 assessments in 2025**.

*Unless you need a printed version as part of reasonable adjustments for particular needs, in which case you must discuss this with your tutor at least six weeks before the assessment date.

# Contents

# 1.    Rates of VAT

**Taxable supplies:**

| | |
|---|---|
| **Standard rate** | 20% |
| **Reduced rate** | 5% |
| **Zero rate** | 0% |

**Non-taxable supplies have no VAT applied:**

- Exempt
- Outside the scope of VAT

# 2.    Registration and deregistration for VAT

| | |
|---|---|
| Registration threshold | £90,000 |
| Deregistration threshold | £88,000 |

| Compulsory registration | Notify HMRC | Registration effective from |
|---|---|---|
| Historic test | Within 30 days of the end of the month threshold was exceeded | First day of the second month after threshold exceeded |
| Future test | Before the end of the 30 day period | From the start of the 30 day period |

| Deregistration | Notify HMRC | Deregistration effective from |
|---|---|---|
| Compulsory | Within 30 days of the business ceasing to make taxable supplies | Date of cessation |
| Voluntary | Evidence that taxable supplies will not exceed the VAT deregistration threshold in the next 12 months | Date request received by HMRC, or Agreed later date |

# 3. Failure to register for VAT

- This can result in a penalty for failure to notify. The penalty is a % of potential lost revenue (PLR).

| Type of behaviour | Within 12 months of tax being due | | 12 months or more after tax was due | |
|---|---|---|---|---|
| | unprompted | prompted | unprompted | prompted |
| Non-deliberate | 0-30% | 10-30% | 10-30% | 20-30% |
| Deliberate but not concealed | 20-70% | 35-70% | 20-70% | 35-70% |
| Deliberate and concealed | 30-100% | 50-100% | 30-100% | 50-100% |

- Penalties will not be applied if there is a reasonable excuse.

- HMRC will treat the business as though it had registered on time and will expect VAT to be accounted for as if it had been charged. The business has two choices:

    i. treat the invoices as VAT inclusive and absorb the VAT which should have been charged, or

    ii. account for VAT as an addition to the charges already invoiced and attempt to recover this VAT from its customers.

# 4. Changes to the VAT registration

HMRC must be notified of a change of:

| | |
|---|---|
| Name, trading name or address | Within 30 days |
| Partnership members | Within 30 days |
| Agent's details | Within 30 days |
| Bank account details | 14 days in advance |
| Change in business activity | Within 30 days |

# 5. Keeping business and VAT records

| | |
|---|---|
| Record retention period | 6 years |
| Penalty for failure to keep records | £500 |

---

# 6. Contents of a VAT invoice

**Full VAT invoice**

- a sequential number based on one or more series which uniquely identifies the document
- the time of the supply (tax point)
- the date of issue of the document (where different to the time of supply)
- supplier's name, address, and VAT registration number
- customer's name and address
- a description sufficient to identify the goods or services supplied
- for each description, the quantity of the goods or the extent of the services, the rate of VAT, and the amount payable excluding VAT — this can be expressed in any currency
- the gross total amount payable, excluding VAT — this can be expressed in any currency
- the rate of any cash discount offered
- the total amount of VAT chargeable — this must be expressed in sterling
- the unit price (applicable to countable elements).

**Simplified VAT invoices (<£250)**

- suppliers name, address, and VAT registration number
- the time of supply (tax point)
- a description which identifies the goods or services supplied
- for each applicable VAT rate, the total amount payable, including VAT  and the VAT rate.

**Modified VAT invoices**

- a full VAT invoice showing the VAT inclusive rather than VAT exclusive values.

# 7. Partial exemption for VAT

| De minimis amount | £625 per month |
|---|---|
| Proportion of total input VAT | <50% |

- Generally, a partially exempt business cannot reclaim the input tax paid on purchases that relate to exempt supplies.

- If the amount of input tax incurred relating to exempt supplies is below a minimum de minimis amount, input tax can be reclaimed in full.

- If the amount of input tax incurred relating to exempt supplies is above the de minimis amount, only the part of the input tax that related to non-exempt supplies can be reclaimed.

# 8. International trade and VAT

| Export of goods | Zero-rated |
| --- | --- |
| Import of goods | UK VAT applied using postponed accounting. |
| Export of services | Apply UK VAT if place of supply is in the UK:<br><br>• for supplies to business, place of supply is the location of the customer (outside the scope of UK VAT)<br>• for supplies to non-business customers, place of supply is the location of the supplier (charge UK VAT). |
| Import of services | Reverse charge applies |

# 9. Tax points for VAT

| Basic tax point date | Date of despatch of the goods/carrying out of the service |
| --- | --- |
| Actual tax point date may be earlier | If either:<br>• payment is received earlier<br>• invoice is issued earlier.<br>Actual tax point becomes the earlier of these two dates. |
| Actual tax point date may be later | If:<br>• invoice is issued within 14 days of despatch/service (and advance payment didn't apply). |

- Deposits are treated separately to final payment and so may have a different tax point.
- The tax point is always the date of payment if cash basis is being applied.
- Where services are being supplied on a continuous basis over a period in excess of a month but invoices are being issued regularly throughout the period, a tax point is created every time an invoice is issued or a payment is made, whichever happens first.
- Goods on sale or return will have a tax point date either on adoption (the customer indicates they will keep the goods) or 12 months after removal of the goods where this is earlier.

# 10. Time limits for issuing a VAT invoice

Within 30 days of tax point which is either:

- within 30 days of date of supply or
- within 30 days of payment if payment was in advance.

# 11. Blocked expenses and VAT

Input VAT cannot be recovered on blocked expenses.

Business entertainment

- The exception is that input tax can be reclaimed in respect of entertaining overseas customers, but not UK or Isle of Man customers.

- When the entertainment is in respect of a mixed group of both employees and non-employees (e.g. customers and/or suppliers), the business can only reclaim VAT on the proportion of the expenses that is for employees and on the proportion for overseas customers.

**Cars**

- Input VAT can only be recovered on cars if it is wholly for business (no private use).

- 50% of input VAT can be recovered when cars are hired/leased.

- VAT can be recovered on commercial vehicles such as vans/lorries.

**Assets with private use**

- The VAT recovery should be based only on the proportion related to business use.

# 12. Fuel scale charge and VAT

If the business pays for road fuel, it can deal with the VAT charged on the fuel in one of four ways:

- reclaim all of the VAT. All of the fuel must be used only for business purposes

- reclaim all of the VAT and pay the appropriate fuel scale charge (as follows) - this is a way of accounting for output tax on fuel that the business buys but that is then used for private motoring

- reclaim only the VAT that relates to fuel used for business mileage. Detailed records of business and private mileage must be kept

- do not reclaim any VAT. This can be a useful option if mileage is low and also if fuel is used for both business and private motoring. If the business chooses this option, it must apply it to all vehicles, including commercial vehicles.

The fuel scale charge is as follows:

| Description of vehicle: vehicle's CO2 emissions figure | VAT inclusive consideration for a 12 month prescribed accounting period (£) | VAT inclusive consideration for a 3 month prescribed accounting period (£) | VAT inclusive consideration for a 1 month prescribed accounting period (£) |
|---|---|---|---|
| 120 or less | 702 | 174 | 58 |
| 125 | 1,050 | 263 | 87 |
| 130 | 1,123 | 279 | 92 |
| 135 | 1,191 | 297 | 98 |
| 140 | 1,263 | 315 | 105 |
| 145 | 1,331 | 332 | 110 |
| 150 | 1,404 | 350 | 116 |
| 155 | 1,471 | 368 | 122 |
| 160 | 1,544 | 385 | 127 |
| 165 | 1,612 | 403 | 134 |
| 170 | 1,685 | 420 | 139 |
| 175 | 1,752 | 437 | 145 |
| 180 | 1,825 | 455 | 151 |
| 185 | 1,893 | 473 | 157 |
| 190 | 1,965 | 490 | 163 |
| 195 | 2,033 | 508 | 169 |
| 200 | 2,106 | 526 | 174 |

| Description of vehicle: vehicle's CO2 emissions figure | VAT inclusive consideration for a 12 month prescribed accounting period (£) | VAT inclusive consideration for a 3 month prescribed accounting period (£) | VAT inclusive consideration for a 1 month prescribed accounting period (£) |
|---|---|---|---|
| 205 | 2,174 | 544 | 180 |
| 210 | 2,246 | 560 | 186 |
| 215 | 2,314 | 578 | 192 |
| 220 | 2,387 | 596 | 198 |
| 225 or more | 2,454 | 613 | 203 |

- Where the $CO_2$ emission figure is not a multiple of 5, the figure is rounded down to the next multiple of 5 to determine the level of the charge.

## 13. Bad debt and VAT

VAT that has been paid to HMRC and which has not been received from the customer can be reclaimed as bad debt relief. The conditions are that:

    i.    the debt is more than six months and less than four years and six months old

    ii.    the debt has been written off in the VAT account and transferred to a separate bad debt account

    iii.    the debt has not been sold or handed to a factoring company

    iv.    the business did not charge more than the normal selling price for the items.

Bad debt relief does not apply when the cash accounting scheme is used because the VAT is not paid to HMRC until after the customer has paid it to the supplier.

# 14. Due dates for submitting the VAT return and paying electronically

| | |
|---|---|
| Deadline for submitting return and paying VAT – quarterly accounting | 1 month and 7 days after the end of the VAT period |
| Deadline if being paid by direct debit | HMRC will collect 3 working days after the submission deadline. |

- Please see alternative submission and payment deadlines for special accounting schemes.

# 15. Special accounting schemes for VAT

## 15.1 Annual accounting scheme for VAT

| | | |
|---|---|---|
| Joining the scheme | Maximum (estimated) taxable turnover in the next 12 months | £1.35m |
| Leaving the scheme | Compulsory if taxable turnover at the end of the VAT accounting year exceeds the threshold | £1.6m |
| VAT returns | One annual return | 2 months after the end of the accounting period |
| VAT payments (monthly) | Nine monthly interim payments (10% of estimated VAT bill based on previous returns) | At the end of months 4 to 12 in the accounting period |
| | Balancing payment | 2 months after the end of the accounting period |
| VAT payments (quarterly) | Three interim payments (25% of estimated VAT bill based on previous returns) | At the end of months 4, 7 and 10 in the accounting period |
| | Balancing payment | 2 months after the end of the accounting period |

## 15.2 Cash accounting scheme for VAT

| | | |
|---|---|---|
| Joining the scheme | Maximum (estimated) taxable turnover in the next 12 months | £1.35m |
| Leaving the scheme | Compulsory if taxable turnover at the end of the VAT accounting year exceeds the threshold | £1.6m |
| Deadlines for submission and payment | | Same as normal scheme |

## 15.3 Flat rate scheme for VAT

| | | |
|---|---|---|
| Joining the scheme | Maximum taxable turnover (excluding VAT) in the next 12 months | £150,000 |
| Leaving the scheme | On the anniversary of joining, maximum turnover in the last 12 months (including VAT) or expected turnover in next 12 months | £230,000 |
| Discount | In first year of being VAT-registered | 1% |
| Limited cost business | Goods cost less than either:<br><br>• 2% of turnover, or<br>• £1,000 a year | 16.5% |
| Capital expenditure | Input tax can be recovered on individual large capital purchases | £2,000 |
| Deadlines for submission and payment | | Same as normal scheme |

• The appropriate flat rate % will be provided in the assessment.

# 16. Errors in previous VAT returns

Adjustments can be made to correct net errors that are:

- below the reporting threshold
- not deliberate
- for an accounting period that ended less than 4 years ago.

The reporting threshold is;

- £10,000 or less or
- for net errors between £10,000 and £50,000, up to 1% of the Box 6 figure (total value of sales and all other outputs excluding any VAT) for the period in which the error was discovered

When the next VAT return is submitted, the net value of errors is added to VAT due on sales and other outputs for tax due to HMRC, or to VAT reclaimed in the period on purchases and other inputs for tax due to the business.

If the value of the net VAT error discovered is above the reporting threshold, it must be declared to HMRC separately, in writing.

# 17. Late submission and late payment of VAT

## 17.1 Late submission

| Submission frequency | Penalty point threshold | Period of compliance |
|---|---|---|
| Annual | 2 points | 24 months |
| Quarterly | 4 points | 12 months |

| | |
|---|---|
| Initial penalty | £200 |
| Subsequent penalty | £200 |

## Removal of penalty points

| | |
|---|---|
| **Business has not reached penalty threshold** | When penalty points expire depends on the date the VAT return was due. |
| | If the deadline for the VAT return was: |
| | • not the last day of a month — a penalty point expires on the last day of the month, 24 months after this |
| | • the last day of a month — a penalty point expires on the last day of the month, 25 months after this |
| **Business has reached penalty threshold** | All points will be reset to zero if both conditions below are met: |
| | • a period of compliance (meeting all submission obligations on time for the period of compliance), and |
| | • all submissions due in the preceding 24 months have been made (whether or not they were on time). |

## 17.2 Late payment

| Number of days overdue | First late payment penalty | Second late payment penalty |
|---|---|---|
| **up to 15** | None | None |
| **16 to 30** | 2% on the VAT outstanding at day 15 | None |
| **31 or more** | 2% on the VAT outstanding at day 15<br><br>AND<br><br>2% on the VAT outstanding at day 30 | A daily rate based on 4% per annum charged every day from day 31 until paid in full |

### 17.3  Interest charged

Interest is calculated at the Bank of England base rate plus 2.5%.

The Bank of England base rate will be given in the assessment.

# 18.  Assessment of VAT

If a VAT Return is not submitted on time, HMRC will issue a 'VAT notice of assessment of tax' which will state how much HMRC think is owed.

If HMRC issue an assessment that is too low, a penalty of up to 30% can be charged for not telling them it is incorrect within 30 days.

# 19.  Penalties for inaccuracies in VAT return

A penalty can be charged as a percentage of the potential lost revenue (PLR):

| Type of behaviour | Unprompted disclosure % | Prompted disclosure % |
|---|---|---|
| Careless | 0 - 30 | 15 - 30 |
| Deliberate | 20 - 70 | 35 - 70 |
| Deliberate and concealed | 30 - 100 | 50 - 100 |

# 20.  Payroll record retention

| Retention period | 3 years from end of tax year |
|---|---|
| Penalty for failure to maintain records | £3,000 |

# 21.  Types of payroll submission

**Full Payment Submission (FPS)**

- File on or before employees pay day.
- Include payments to and deductions for all employees.

**Employer Payment Summary (EPS)**

- File if no employees were paid in the month.
- Send by the 19th of the following tax month.

## 22. Payroll deadlines

| | |
|---|---|
| Registering for PAYE | You must register before the first payday. You cannot register more than 2 months before you start paying people |
| Month end date for PAYE | 5th of each month |
| Payment date for monthly payroll | 22nd of the following month if paid electronically. 19th otherwise. If monthly amounts are <£1,500, quarterly payments can be made |
| Provide employees with P60 | 31st May following the end of the tax year |
| Filing deadline for Expenses & Benefits forms | 6th July following the end of the tax year |
| Class 1A NIC payment date | 22nd July following the end of the tax year, if paying electronically. 19th July following the end of the tax year, otherwise. |

## 23. Penalties for late submission of payroll filings

Penalties may apply if:
- the FPS was late
- the expected amount of FPSs was not filed
- an EPS was not filed.

| Number of employees | Monthly penalty |
|---|---|
| 1 to 9 | £100 |
| 10 to 49 | £200 |
| 50 to 249 | £300 |
| 250 or more | £400 |

Penalties may not apply if:

- the FPS is late but all reported payments on the FPS are within three days of the employees' payday (unless there is regular lateness)
- a new employer is late but sends the first FPS within 30 days of paying an employee
- it is a business's first failure in the tax year to send a report on time.

# 24. Penalties for late payroll payment

**Late payment of monthly/quarterly payments**
- The first failure to pay in a tax year does not count as a default.
- Late payment penalties apply to late payments and payments of less than is due.

| Number of defaults in a tax year | Penalty percentage applied to the amount that is late in the relevant tax month |
|---|---|
| 1 to 3 | 1% |
| 4 to 6 | 2% |
| 7 to 9 | 3% |
| 10 or more | 4% |

Additional penalties will apply if:

| | |
|---|---|
| A monthly or quarterly amount remains outstanding after 6 months | 5% of unpaid tax |
| A monthly or quarterly amount remains outstanding after 12 months | A further 5% of unpaid tax |

These additional penalties apply even where only one payment in the tax year is late.

**Late payments of amounts due annually or occasionally**

| | |
|---|---|
| 30 days late | 5% |
| 6 months late | Additional 5% |
| 12 months late | Additional 5% |

# 25. Penalties for inaccuracies in payroll filings

A penalty can be charged as a percentage of the potential lost revenue (PLR):

| Type of behaviour | Unprompted disclosure % | Prompted disclosure % |
|---|---|---|
| Careless | 0 - 30 | 15 - 30 |
| Deliberate | 20 - 70 | 35 - 70 |
| Deliberate and concealed | 30 - 100 | 50 - 100 |

AAT
30 Churchill Place
London E14 5RE

**aat.org.uk**

# Section 1

# PRACTICE QUESTIONS

## VAT PRINCIPLES, REGISTRATION AND DEREGISTRATION AND SPECIAL SCHEMES

**Key answer tips**

Tasks will usually have a number of parts. Some of the questions in this section of the kit are multi-part whereas others give practice on the individual parts likely to be tested in this type of task.

Areas covered are some of the basics of VAT, particularly the registration conditions, registration and deregistration thresholds as well as information on the special schemes.

## 1 HUGH

(a) **Which TWO of the following statements are true?**

(i) Hugh need not register for VAT if he has made taxable supplies of £91,000 in the last 12 months but expects his taxable supplies in the next 12 months to be £89,000.

(ii) A business has made £91,000 of taxable supplies in the last 12 months including £10,000 of sales of capital assets previously used by the business. The business is not required to register at this time.

(iii) A business which exceeds the registration threshold under the historic test on 31 July will be required to notify HMRC by 30 August and will be registered with effect from 1 September.

(iv) A business that expects to make taxable supplies of £91,000 in the next 30 days must notify HMRC by the end of the 30-day period and will be registered with effect from the end of the 30-day period.

A    (i) and (ii)

B    (ii) and (iii)

C    (iii) and (iv)

D    (i) and (iv)

(b)     Can the following VAT-registered traders deregister their business <u>voluntarily</u>?

Tick one box on EACH line.

|  | Yes | No |
|---|---|---|
| A business that is ceasing to trade. |  |  |
| A continuing business that expects to make supplies of £88,000 in the next year of which one quarter will be exempt supplies. |  |  |
| A business that expects to make taxable supplies of £89,000 in the next 12 months. |  |  |
| A continuing business which has been making taxable supplies of £92,000 per year but which has now switched to making wholly exempt supplies of the same amount. |  |  |

## 2     JENKINS

Jenkins runs or part runs the following five businesses:

|  | Taxable supplies per year |
|---|---|
| Three sole trader businesses | £40,000 each |
| A business run in partnership with his wife | £100,000 |
| A business run in partnership with his wife and brother | £95,000 |

(a)     How many separate VAT registrations are required to cover these businesses?

A     2

B     3

C     4

D     5

(b)     Which of the following statements is incorrect?  Select ONE answer.

A     Only registered businesses can charge VAT to customers.

B     VAT is a charge which is ultimately suffered by the end consumer.

C     A business making £60,000 of exempt supplies and £20,000 of zero-rated supplies cannot register for VAT.

D     Many VAT queries can be answered by referring to the HMRC website.

**3    NASSER**

Nasser is thinking of registering his business for VAT voluntarily rather than waiting until his taxable turnover is over the registration threshold.

(a)    **Which TWO of the following reasons might explain why a business would not voluntarily register for VAT?**

Tick the two correct reasons.

| | Would not voluntarily register |
|---|---|
| It makes their goods more expensive for other VAT-registered businesses. | |
| It makes their goods more expensive for businesses that are not VAT-registered. | |
| It helps to avoid penalties for late registration. | |
| It increases the business burden of administration. | |

(b)    **What does Nasser need to demonstrate to HMRC to be able to register voluntarily? Select ONE answer.**

A    That he needs to be able to recover his input tax to make his business successful

B    That he intends to make only exempt supplies

C    That he intends to make only zero-rated supplies

D    That he intends to make either zero-rated or standard-rated supplies or both

**4    ISY**

Isy started a business on 1 December. Her monthly sales are £12,300 split equally between standard-rated, zero-rated and exempt supplies.

(a)    **On what date will she exceed the compulsory VAT registration threshold?**

A    Never

B    31 July

C    31 October

D    30 November

Jo runs a small sole trader business which is registered for VAT. Her business is taken over as a going concern by another sole trader, Dorrit. Dorrit runs a similar business that is currently not registered for VAT. The combined turnover of the new business will be £190,000.

(b)    **Can the VAT registration of Jo's business be transferred across to the new combined business?**                                                                    **YES/NO**

## 5 DOOKU

Dooku is considering the purchase of one of the following unregistered businesses.

**For each business, if he did purchase the business should he register it for VAT immediately, or monitor turnover and register later?**

Tick one box on EACH line.

| | Register now | Monitor and register later |
|---|---|---|
| A business with £50,000 of taxable turnover in the last 11 months but which expects taxable turnover of £92,000 in the next 30 days. | | |
| A business with taxable turnover of £5,000 per month for the last 12 months. | | |
| A business with taxable turnover of £7,950 per month for the last 12 months. | | |
| A business with turnover of standard-rated supplies of £4,000 per month for the last year but which expects turnover of £50,000 in the next 30 days. | | |

## 6 CERTIFICATE OF REGISTRATION

**(a)    Why is a VAT certificate of registration important?**

Choose ONE answer.

A    It is proof that the business has started to trade

B    It is proof that the business is entitled to charge output VAT

C    It is proof of the trader's VAT registration number

D    It is proof that the business makes taxable supplies

**(b)    Which of the following are powers of HMRC in respect of VAT?**

Tick one box on each line.

| | Is a power | Is not a power |
|---|---|---|
| Charging penalties for breaches of VAT rules | | |
| Completing VAT returns | | |
| Inspecting premises | | |
| Providing suitable books for VAT record keeping | | |
| Changing the rate of VAT | | |

**(c)** **Identify which ONE of the following statements is correct about UK VAT legislation and administration.**

A    HMRC is the relevant tax authority for VAT other than in Wales and Scotland.

B    HMRC passes VAT laws and issues guidance to interpret these.

C    Registered businesses pay VAT collected from consumers to their local councils.

D    Consumers, the final users of taxable supplies, cannot recover VAT from HMRC.

**7    REMONA**

**(a)    Which one of the following statements is correct?**

Select ONE answer.

A    Remona should have registered on 1 September but did not register. Since that time, she has invoiced sales of standard-rated goods totalling £15,000. She will be liable for output VAT of £3,000.

B    The taxable turnover for the historic registration test can be measured at any time, not just the end of the month.

C    When a trader fails to register on time, they can be charged a penalty of up to 100% of the tax due.

D    All registered traders submit VAT returns quarterly.

**(b)    Identify whether each of the following statements about VAT records is true or false.**

Tick one box for EACH line.

|  | True | False |
|---|---|---|
| Paper copies of electronic VAT records must be kept, in case of computer failure. |  |  |
| VAT records must be kept for six years. |  |  |
| A VAT-registered business must keep digital VAT records. |  |  |
| The maximum penalty for not keeping VAT records is 100% of the VAT due per those records. |  |  |

**8    TROI**

Troi has a business which makes standard-rated and zero-rated supplies but is not yet registered for VAT.

She has given you the following details about her sales.

|  | Monthly turnover | |
|---|---|---|
|  | Standard-rated | Zero-rated |
|  | £ | £ |
| Year ended 31 December 2024 | 2,500 | 4,000 |
| January 2025 | 3,500 | 4,100 |
| February 2025 | 7,500 | 5,600 |
| March 2025 | 8,900 | 6,200 |
| April 2025 and thereafter | 8,700 | 5,900 |

(a) **At the end of which month does Troi exceed the registration threshold?**

    A    February 2025

    B    March 2025

    C    April 2025

    D    December 2025

(b) **Which of the following statements on the subject of cash accounting are true?**

Select TWO answers.

    A    Input VAT is reclaimed by reference to the date the supplier is paid.

    B    Traders can join the scheme provided their annual taxable turnover does not exceed £1,600,000.

    C    VAT invoices do not need to be sent to customers.

    D    Arthur is a VAT-registered trader whose annual turnover excluding VAT is £400,000. He has never had any convictions for VAT offences. He is eligible to join the cash accounting scheme.

## 9 ANNUAL ACCOUNTING

(a) **What is the turnover threshold for eligibility to join the annual accounting scheme?**

    A    Estimated turnover in the next 12 months is not more than £150,000.

    B    Estimated turnover in the next 12 months is not more than £230,000.

    C    Estimated turnover in the next 12 months is not more than £1,350,000.

    D    Estimated turnover in the next 12 months is not more than £1,600,000.

With the annual accounting scheme, one VAT return is made each year.

(b) **How many months after the end of the accounting period end is the return due?**

    A    1 month

    B    2 months

    C    3 months

    D    1 year

Exe Ltd is a company that sells children's clothing. This is a zero-rated activity.

(c) **Is Exe Ltd likely to benefit from joining the annual accounting scheme?**

    A    Yes

    B    No

PRACTICE QUESTIONS: **SECTION 1**

Queue Ltd is a VAT-registered business whose turnover of taxable supplies has been declining for several years.

**(d)   Is Queue likely to benefit from joining the annual accounting scheme?**

A   Yes

B   No

**(e)   Identify ONE occasion when a trader using the annual accounting scheme must leave the scheme.**

A   The taxable turnover (excluding VAT) has exceeded £1,350,000 in a VAT year

B   The taxable turnover (excluding VAT) has exceeded £1,600,000 in a VAT year

C   The taxable turnover (including VAT) has exceeded £1,350,000 in a VAT year

D   The taxable turnover (including VAT) has exceeded £1,600,000 in a VAT year

## 10   ZED LTD

Zed Ltd is a company that uses the annual accounting scheme for VAT with monthly payments. Its VAT liability for the previous accounting period was £72,900.

**(a)   What is its monthly payment on account for the current year?**

A   12 monthly payments of £6,075

B   12 monthly payments of £5,468

C   9 monthly payments of £7,290

D   9 monthly payments of £8,100

Laredo is a VAT-registered trader who has adopted the cash accounting scheme. He receives an order from a customer on 13 March and despatches the goods on 20 March. He invoices the customer on 24 March and receives payment on 2 May.

**(b)   What is the tax point date?**

A   13 March

B   20 March

C   24 March

D   2 May

KAPLAN PUBLISHING                                                                                  7

## 11    TARAN

Taran runs a VAT-registered business and needs more information about the annual accounting scheme.

**(a)    Which of the following statements are true and which false?**

Tick one box for EACH line.

|  | True | False |
|---|---|---|
| Taxpayers must be up-to-date with their VAT payments before they are allowed to join the scheme. |  |  |
| Monthly payments on account are 10% of the previous year's VAT liability. |  |  |
| Monthly payments can be made using any method convenient to the taxpayer. |  |  |
| Monthly payments are made 7 days after the end of the month. |  |  |
| Monthly payments are made at the end of months 2 to 10 in the accounting period. |  |  |
| The scheme allows businesses to budget for their VAT payments more easily. |  |  |

In the last quarter, Dernbach has made sales as follows:

|  | £ |
|---|---|
| Standard-rated sales (including VAT) | 22,470 |
| Zero-rated sales | 4,500 |
| Exempt sales | 1,110 |

The normal flat rate percentage for her type of business is 8%. The business is a limited cost business.

**(b)    What is her VAT payable for the quarter?**

A    £3,707.55

B    £2,246.40

C    £4,633.20

D    £4,015.27

## 12 FLAT RATE SCHEME

(a) **Would the following VAT-registered businesses benefit from joining the flat rate scheme?**

Tick one box on EACH line.

|  | Will benefit | Will not benefit |
|---|---|---|
| A business making solely zero-rated supplies to other businesses. |  |  |
| A business with a lower than average (for their trade sector) level of input tax. |  |  |
| A business with a higher proportion of standard-rated supplies than other businesses in the same trade sector. |  |  |

(b) **Identify which of the following could be reasons why a VAT-registered business uses the flat rate scheme.**

(i) only one VAT return is required each year

(ii) there is automatic relief for bad debts

(iii) monthly fixed VAT payments help cash flow

A None of the above

B (i) only

C (i) and (ii) only

D All of the above

## 13 HACKETT

Hackett joins the flat rate scheme in his first year of VAT registration. His sales for the first quarter are as follows:

|  | £ |
|---|---|
| Standard-rated sales (excluding VAT) | 18,600 |
| Exempt sales | 2,400 |

The normal flat rate percentage for his type of business is 11%. The business is not a limited cost business.

(a) **What is his VAT payable for the quarter?**

A £2,310.00

B £2,719.20

C £2,232.00

D £2,472.00

Ray makes the following statements about the flat rate scheme.

**(b)** **Which of the statements are true and which false?**

Tick one box on EACH line.

| | True | False |
|---|---|---|
| A business can join the flat rate scheme provided its taxable turnover for the next 12 months is expected to be less than £230,000. | | |
| VAT due to HMRC is calculated as a fixed percentage of VAT-inclusive taxable turnover. | | |
| VAT is shown on invoices calculated at the flat rate percentage. | | |
| A business can be in both the flat rate scheme and the annual accounting scheme at the same time. | | |
| The scheme cuts down on the time spent on VAT administration. | | |
| Businesses cannot pay less VAT under the flat rate scheme than the normal method of accounting for VAT. | | |

# CALCULATING AND ACCOUNTING FOR VAT

**Key answer tips**

Tasks will usually have two or three parts. Some of the questions in this section of the kit are multi-part whereas others give practice on the individual parts likely to be tested in this area.

Candidates are expected to know about VAT invoices and their content, the use of simplified invoices and modified invoices and the tax point for each supply.

**14 CAIN**

Cain runs a VAT-registered business. On 4 May, he receives an order for goods from a customer. On 15 May, the goods are delivered and on 20 May, Cain issues a tax invoice. The customer pays on 28 June.

**(a)** **What is the tax point date?**

A    4 May

B    15 May

C    20 May

D    28 June

Clarence is a VAT-registered trader. He receives an order from a customer on 17 August. Payment is received on 20 August and the goods are delivered on 24 August. A VAT invoice is sent to the customer on 31 August.

**(b)     What is the tax point date?**

    A       17 August

    B       20 August

    C       24 August

    D       31 August

Drogba is a VAT-registered trader. He receives an order for standard-rated goods on 1 February, delivers the goods to the customer on 7 February, sends a tax invoice on 28 February, and receives payment on 19 March.

**(c)     What is the tax point date?**

    A       1 February

    B       7 February

    C       28 February

    D       19 March

## 15    RATTAN

Rattan is a VAT-registered trader. She receives an order for standard-rated goods on 11 April, delivers the goods to the customer on 19 April, sends an invoice on 8 May, and receives payment on 24 May.

**(a)     What is the tax point date?**

    A       11 April

    B       19 April

    C       8 May

    D       24 May

Sisal runs a VAT-registered business. He received an order from a customer on 13 October. He delivered the goods to the customer on 24 October and issued a tax invoice on 29 October. The customer paid for the goods on 6 December.

**(b)     What is the tax point date?**

    A       13 October

    B       24 October

    C       29 October

    D       6 December

Reed is a VAT-registered trader. He receives a deposit from a customer on 16 July. The goods are delivered to the customer on 24 July and a VAT invoice is sent to the customer on 4 August. The customer settles the balance of the invoice on 2 September.

(c)    **What is the tax point date in respect of the deposit?**

   A    16 July

   B    24 July

   C    4 August

   D    2 September

## 16    ROGER

Roger is registered for VAT and all of his supplies are standard-rated. He requires a 20% deposit from his customers within 10 days of receiving an order.

(a)    **What are the tax points for the deposit and the balance in each of the following?**

Complete the table with the appropriate dates.

| Deposit paid | Goods delivered | Invoice raised | Balance paid | Tax point for deposit | Tax point for balance |
|---|---|---|---|---|---|
| 10 March | 12 March | 30 March | 18 March | | |
| 21 February | 7 March | 10 March | 1 April | | |
| 13 May | 26 May | 11 June | 7 July | | |

(b)    **Which of the statements are true and which false?**

Tick one box on EACH line.

| | True | False |
|---|---|---|
| A pro-forma invoice is a valid tax invoice. | | |
| A customer receiving a pro-forma invoice can use it to reclaim the input tax shown. | | |
| A modified invoice includes all the same details as a full invoice. | | |
| Traders do not have to supply a VAT invoice unless their customer is VAT registered. | | |

## 17 BOLD

Bold is a VAT-registered trader who makes a mixture of standard-rated and zero-rated supplies. He makes a wholly zero-rated supply to Zed Ltd delivering the goods on 20 July and issuing an invoice on 25 July. He receives payment on 31 July.

**(a)    Which of the following statements are true?**

Tick one box for each line.

| | True | False |
|---|---|---|
| The tax point date is 20 July. | | |
| The tax point date is 25 July. | | |
| An invoice for a wholly zero-rated supply is not a tax invoice. | | |
| Input tax recovery in respect of zero-rated supplies is restricted. | | |

This is a shop invoice for a cash purchase.

| Wealdstone Supplies, | |
|---|---|
| 14, Western Rd, | |
| Cleethorpes | |
| VAT registration number: 123 4567 89 | |
| Date: 16 October 2025 | |

| Quantity | | £ |
|---|---|---|
| 1 | Dishwasher | 420.00 |
| | | |
| | Total due | 420.00 |
| | VAT 20% included | Cash paid |

**(b)    Is this a valid VAT invoice?  Select one of the options below.**

A    Yes, it is a valid VAT invoice.

B    Yes, it is a valid simplified VAT invoice.

C    Neither of the above.

## 18 MARGARET

Margaret is a VAT-registered trader. She receives a supplier credit note and processes it in her quarter ended 30 September.

**(a)    What will be the effect on VAT?**

Choose one answer.

A    Output tax will increase.

B    Output tax will decrease.

C    Input tax will increase.

D    Input tax will decrease.

A UK business issues a sales invoice for taxable supplies of goods to a customer outside the UK.

**(b)**    **What is the effect on VAT for the UK business?**

Choose one answer.

A       Output tax will increase.

B       Output tax will stay the same.

C       Input tax will decrease.

D       Output tax will decrease.

## 19    MARGOT

Margot is having trouble dealing with credit notes and debit notes.

**(a)    She makes the following statements and wants you to tell her which are true and which false.**

Tick one box on EACH line.

| | True | False |
|---|---|---|
| The receipt of a credit note from a supplier will reduce her output tax. | | |
| The issue of a debit note to a supplier will reduce her input tax. | | |
| The issue of a credit note to a customer will reduce her output tax. | | |
| The receipt of a debit note from a customer will reduce her output tax. | | |

Jonsson does not make sales to the public.

**(b)    Which of the following does Jonsson NOT have to include on his sales invoices to other UK businesses?**

A       Name and address of the supplier

B       Name and address of the customer

C       VAT registration number of the customer

D       The tax-exclusive value of the invoice

**(c)    Which of the following does Jackson, a retailer, NOT have to include on his simplified invoices?**

Select one answer.

A       Time of supply

B       Description of each item supplied

C       Rate of VAT applicable to the supply

D       The tax-exclusive value of the invoice

**20   AHMED**

Ahmed is just starting in business and wants his invoices to comply with VAT rules. He gives you the following list of some of the things he is proposing to include.

**(a)   Which items are required for a full VAT invoice?**

Tick one box for each line.

| | Required | Not required |
|---|---|---|
| Time of supply | | |
| Customer order number | | |
| Description of the type of supply | | |
| Rate of VAT applicable | | |
| General terms of trade | | |
| Total amount payable excluding VAT | | |
| Total amount of VAT payable | | |
| Acceptable methods of payment | | |

Chen is a VAT-registered trader. He issues a sales credit note to a customer.

**(b)   What will be the effect on VAT?**

Choose one answer.

A   Input tax will increase.

B   Input tax will decrease.

C   Output tax will increase.

D   Output tax will decrease.

Wing is a VAT-registered trader. He receives a supplier credit note.

**(c)   What effect will this have on the amount of VAT due to HMRC?**

Choose one answer.

A   The amount payable will decrease.

B   The amount payable will increase.

**21   EFFIE**

Effie wishes to issue simplified invoices.

**(a)   What is the invoice limit above which simplified invoices cannot be issued?**

A   £50

B   £100

C   £200

D   £250

Alice, who is a retailer, issues detailed and simplified invoices.

**(b)  Which invoice copies should she keep?**

    A     Simplified invoices only

    B     Detailed invoices only

    C     Both

    D     Neither

Jordanne sells goods on a sale or return basis.

Goods are delivered on a sale or return basis to a customer on 6 May 2024.

The customer does not formally notify Jordanne that they wish to keep the goods but sends a payment for them on 12 August 2024.

Jordanne issues an invoice to the customer on 31 August 2024.

**(c)  What is the tax point date in respect of these goods?**

    A     6 May 2024

    B     12 August 2024

    C     31 August 2024

    D     6 May 2025

## 22  SALLY

**(a)  Sally wants to know if she can issue simplified invoices for the following supplies.**

Tick one box on EACH line. All figures are VAT-exclusive.

| | Can be issued | Cannot be issued |
|---|---|---|
| Standard-rated supplies of £210 | | |
| Standard-rated supplies of £170 plus zero-rated supplies of £40 | | |

Finian sells a number of capital assets over the year.

**(b)  Complete the table to show the amount of output VAT that must be charged on the sale of each item.**

| Item | Input tax recovered | Sale proceeds (excluding VAT) | Output VAT |
|---|---|---|---|
| | | £ | £.pp |
| Computer | Yes | 400 | |
| Car | Yes | 7,500 | |
| Van | Yes | 6,100 | |
| Car | No | 8,400 | |

## 23 SCOTTY

Scotty sells goods on a sale or return basis. Customers have to pay a deposit of 10% of the cost of the goods, which is refunded if the goods are returned within six months.

A customer pays a 10% deposit on 2 March and receives the goods on a sale or return basis on 4 March.

On 10 June, they notify Scotty that they wish to keep the goods.

Scotty issues an invoice dated 21 June and receives the remaining 90% of the cost on 11 July.

**(a)** **Which one of the following statements is true?**

A   There are two tax points: one on 2 March for 10% of the cost, and one on 10 June for the remaining 90%.

B   There are two tax points: one on 2 March for 10% of the cost, and one on 21 June for the remaining 90%.

C   There is one tax point on 10 June.

D   There is one tax point on 21 June.

Nasheen is a VAT-registered trader who has made the following sales of standard-rated items in the previous month.

|  | £ |
|---|---|
| To AB Ltd (amount inclusive of VAT) | 562 |
| To XY plc (amount exclusive of VAT) | 750 |

**(b)** **What is the total output tax on these two supplies?**

A   £262.40

B   £218.66

C   £237.40

D   £243.66

## 24 KIM

Kim provides accountancy services.

On 15 November, he commences preparing financial statements for a client and finishes this work on 3 December.

He issues an invoice to the client on 18 December and receives payment on 29 December.

**(a)** **What is the tax point date in respect of these services?**

A   15 November

B   3 December

C   18 December

D   29 December

**(b)** **Identify which of the following Nisha, a retailer, does NOT have to include on her modified invoices.**

Select one answer.

A      The tax-inclusive value of the invoice

B      The tax-exclusive value of the invoice

C      The total amount of VAT

D      The customer's VAT registration number

## 25  BYRON

Byron runs a business leasing plant and machinery to customers for periods of 2 to 4 years. At the end of the lease period the plant and machinery is returned to Byron.

Customers pay a regular monthly amount by direct debit on the 20th of each month.

**(a)** **Which of the following statements are true and which false?**

Tick one box on each line.

| | True | False |
|---|---|---|
| If Byron invoices his customers on the last day of each month, then that day will be the tax point. | | |
| If Byron invoices his customers on the last day of each month, then the tax point will be the 20th of each month. | | |
| Byron can invoice his customers annually in advance, setting out the schedule of payments for the year. If he does this, his customers will be able to recover input tax for the year on receipt of that invoice, as the invoice date will be the tax point. | | |
| Byron can invoice his customers annually in advance, setting out the schedule of payments for the year. If he does this, there will be twelve separate monthly tax points. | | |

Dinah is a VAT-registered trader. She made a supply of £4,200 inclusive of VAT at the reduced rate, and a standard-rated supply of £1,000 exclusive of VAT.

**(b)** **What is the total output tax on these supplies?**

A      £376.67

B      £400.00

C      £410.00

D      £900.00

# RECOVERY OF INPUT TAX

**Key answer tips**

Tasks will usually have a number of parts. Some of the questions in this section of the kit are multi-part whereas others give practice on the individual parts likely to be tested in this type of task.

In these tasks, the candidates' knowledge of the rules regarding when input tax can be recovered will be tested.

Questions will test the learners' knowledge of the impact of a trader being classed as partially exempt, the effect of the fuel scale charge and items on which input tax cannot be recovered.

## 26 PUCK

Puck's business is VAT-registered and supplies goods that are a mix of standard-rated and exempt.

For a VAT quarter, 85% of Puck's supplies (exclusive of VAT) were standard-rated supplies. The remaining 15% were exempt supplies.

The total input tax for the quarter was £15,000, of which £13,000 related to standard-rated supplies and £2,000 to exempt supplies.

(a)   **Identify which of the following statements is true about the input tax reclaimable for the quarter.**

   A    None of the input tax can be reclaimed

   B    Only 85% of the input tax can be reclaimed

   C    Only £13,000 of the input tax can be reclaimed

   D    All the input tax can be reclaimed as the portion relating to exempt supplies is less than 50%

Forte runs a manufacturing business which makes only standard-rated supplies. During March, the business incurs expenditure of £890 on staff entertaining, £456 on UK customer entertaining and £9,150 on a second hand van. All figures include VAT at 20%.

(b)   **What input VAT can be claimed in respect of these three items?**

   A    £1,749.33

   B    £1,673.33

   C    £1,601.00

   D    £2,008.00

**27    JERRY**

Jerry is confused about the difference between making zero-rated and exempt supplies.

**He makes the following statements and wants you to tell him which are true and which false.**

Tick one box on EACH line.

| | True | False |
|---|---|---|
| Traders who make only exempt supplies cannot register for VAT. | | |
| Traders who only make zero-rated supplies have to register for VAT. | | |
| Zero-rated supplies made by a registered trader are not classed as taxable supplies. | | |
| Traders making only exempt supplies cannot recover input tax. | | |
| VAT-registered traders making a mix of zero-rated and exempt supplies cannot recover any input tax. | | |

**28    DONNE**

Donne runs a business in which 70% of her sales are taxable supplies and 30% exempt supplies.

She divides her input tax into three parts: that relating to taxable supplies, that relating to exempt supplies, and that relating to overheads.

**(a)    Select which of the following statements is true.**

A    Only the input tax relating to taxable supplies can be recovered

B    All of the input tax relating to taxable supplies can be recovered. It is also possible to recover 70% of the input tax relating to the exempt supplies and overheads provided this amount does not exceed a de minimis figure

C    Recoverable input tax can only ever comprise that relating to taxable supplies plus 70% of that relating to overheads

D    It is possible to recover all the input tax provided that the input tax relating to exempt supplies plus 30% of the input tax relating to overheads does not exceed the de minimis figure

**(b)** **Vincenzo's business is VAT-registered. During June, it makes the following cash payments.**

Select Yes or No in the right hand box to show whether the input tax can be reclaimed on the next VAT return.

| Description | Net £ | VAT £ | Gross £ | Reclaim input tax? |
|---|---|---|---|---|
| Repairs to machinery | 1,900.00 | 380.00 | 2,280.00 | Yes/No |
| Delivery van | 10,000.00 | 2,000.00 | 12,000.00 | Yes/No |
| UK customer entertaining | 640.00 | 128.00 | 768.00 | Yes/No |
| Overseas customer entertaining | 310.00 | 62.00 | 372.00 | Yes/No |
| Car (pool car with no private use) | 8,400.00 | 1,680.00 | 10,080.00 | Yes/No |

**29   SELDON**

Seldon wishes to claim irrecoverable (bad) debt relief on a sales invoice to Holmes Ltd with VAT of £145.

**(a)   Which of the following are NOT requirements for Seldon to be able to claim VAT irrecoverable (bad) debt relief?**

Select TWO answers.

A     The debt must have been written off in the accounting records for at least three months before the claim is made

B     Seldon has already paid over the output tax of £145 to HMRC

C     Holmes Ltd has been placed into liquidation

D     Six months have passed since the invoice was due for payment

Luigi's business is VAT-registered and supplies goods that are a mix of standard-rated and zero-rated.

**(b)   Which of the following statements is true?**

A     None of the input VAT can be reclaimed

B     All of the input VAT can be reclaimed provided certain conditions are met

C     Some of the input VAT can be reclaimed, in proportion to the different types of supply

D     All of the input VAT can be reclaimed

Hooch Ltd is a VAT-registered business. The sales manager is provided with a company car and fuel which he uses for both business and private purposes.

The car has $CO_2$ emissions of 155 g/km for which the quarterly fuel scale charge is £368. Petrol paid for by the company for the car in the last quarter amounted to £823.50. Both figures are VAT-inclusive.

**(c)   What is the net effect of these on Hooch Ltd's VAT for the quarter?**

A     VAT payable decreases by £91.10

B     VAT payable increases by £75.92

C     VAT payable decreases by £75.92

D     VAT payable decreases by £198.58

## 30 RAFA AND CO

Rafa and Co wish to avoid paying VAT fuel scale charges in respect of employees' motor expenses.

**(a)** **Which of the following mean they still have to pay a VAT scale charge?**

A    The business will only reclaim VAT on fuel used for business mileage and will keep detailed records of business and private mileage driven by employees

B    The business will not reclaim any VAT on fuel

C    The business will only allow employees to claim expenses for fuel for business mileage and will reclaim all input tax on fuel

D    The business will allow employees to claim 50% of their total fuel costs in their expense claims. The business will then reclaim the input tax on these 50% costs

Albert is a registered trader who makes only standard-rated supplies.

In his latest VAT quarter, he has spent £780 on a party for all his staff. Each member of staff brought a guest and exactly half the cost of the party was for these guests. Albert also spent £545 on UK customer entertaining and £10,700 on a second hand lorry.

All figures include VAT.

**(b)** **How much input tax can Albert claim on these costs?**

A    £2,004.16

B    £1,913.33

C    £1,848.33

D    £2,218.00

## 31 VICTORIA LTD

Victoria Ltd provides a car for an employee who uses the car for both business and private purposes. The car has $CO_2$ emissions of 128 g/km. All running expenses of the car are paid for by the company including fuel and the company claims all VAT on the running costs.

**(a)** **Calculate the amount by which output VAT increases per quarter due to the fuel scale charge.**

A    £43.83

B    £46.50

C    £52.60

D    £263.00

Welles is a VAT-registered trader who has not adopted any of the special VAT accounting schemes.

**(b)** **Which one of the following statements about recovery of input tax on the purchase of goods is not true?**

A    Welles needs to have paid for the goods

B    A VAT invoice is usually needed to support the claim

C    The goods or services must be for business use

D    Input tax cannot be recovered on goods used for UK customer entertaining

## 32 MELINDA

Melinda is a VAT-registered trader who has suffered input tax on the following purchases over the last quarter.

(a) **Can Melinda recover input tax on these items?**

Tick one box on EACH line.

| | Recover | Cannot recover |
|---|---|---|
| Purchases for resale | | |
| New laptop computer for Melinda's daughter | | |
| New desk for the office (Melinda has lost the VAT receipt) | | |
| Motorcycle for business deliveries | | |

Kyra makes a taxable supply of widgets at the standard rate. The value of the supply is £900.

A 2% bulk buy discount is offered due to the large quantity ordered on this occasion. A prompt payment discount of 5% is offered for payment within 30 days.

(b) **Assuming the prompt payment discount is taken, calculate the VAT that Kyra must account for on this transaction. Choose one answer.**

A    £180.00

B    £176.40

C    £171.00

D    £167.58

## 33 LARISSA

Larissa is a VAT-registered trader. She sells machine parts with a VAT-exclusive price of £750 to Exe Ltd.

She offers a prompt payment discount of 3% for customers who pay within 21 days.

(a) **What is the correct amount of VAT to be shown on the invoice assuming Larissa adopts the policy of invoicing at the discounted amount?**

A    £150.00

B    £145.50

C    £125.00

D    £121.25

(b) **If the customer pays after 21 days, what is the amount including VAT to be shown on the supplementary invoice to be issued to the customer?**

A    Nil

B    £4.50

C    £22.50

D    £27.00

**34    TRINA**

Trina is a VAT-registered trader who makes a supply of automotive components for £240 to John, which is a standard-rated supply.

Trina offers to pay her customer's VAT on their behalf. Accordingly, John pays £240 to Trina for some automotive parts.

(a)    **What is the correct amount of VAT to be shown on the invoice?**

A    £48.00

B    £40.00

Nawal runs a VAT-registered business. He received an order from a customer on 1 October. He delivered the goods to the customer on 4 October and the customer paid for the goods on 8 October.

(b)    **Identify the date by which Nawal had to issue the VAT invoice.**

A    18 October

B    31 October

C    3 November

D    7 November

# PREPARING, CALCULATING AND ADJUSTING INFORMATION FOR VAT RETURNS

**Key answer tips**

Tasks will usually have a number of parts. Some of the questions in this section of the kit are multi-part whereas others give practice on the individual parts likely to be tested in this type of task.

In this task, learners' understanding of the numbers that appear in a VAT return will be assessed. The task may ask for a calculation of VAT at different rates or awareness of the impact on that VAT return of different events or transactions.

## 35 KEIKO LTD

Keiko Ltd is a business that uses the cash accounting scheme. All sales and purchases are standard-rated.

You are given the following information for the quarter ended 31 May 2025:

|  | £ |
|---|---|
| Sales invoices issued for credit sales | 42,568 |
| Purchase invoices received from suppliers | 29,580 |
| Cash sales receipts | 780 |
| Receipts from customers | 39,745 |
| Cash paid to suppliers | 27,890 |
| Petty cash – purchases of standard-rated items | 175 |

**Calculate the VAT due for the quarter to 31 May 2025. Round down your answer to the nearest penny.**

£

## 36 JULIE

Julie is a VAT-registered trader. During the last quarter, she has made the following sales (all figures are exclusive of VAT).

|  | £ |
|---|---|
| Standard-rated | 40,145 |
| Zero-rated | 21,050 |
| Exempt | 3,450 |
| Sale of used plant (Julie was registered when she purchased this plant) | 5,000 |

**How much output tax should Julie account for in this quarter? Round down your answer to the nearest penny.**

A £7,524.16

B £9,029.00

C £13,239.00

D £8,029.00

**37    AMANDA**

Amanda makes wholly standard-rated supplies. She has reviewed her VAT account and the balance shows that she must pay VAT to HMRC. However, she has forgotten to make the entries listed in the table below.

**Indicate whether the amendment needed to the VAT account will increase, decrease or have no effect on the balance payable to HMRC.**

Tick one box on EACH line.

| | Increases balance payable to HMRC | Decreases balance payable to HMRC | No effect on balance payable to HMRC |
|---|---|---|---|
| VAT on purchases is understated | | | |
| Bad debt relief claim omitted | | | |
| Previous net over claim to be adjusted for on the VAT return omitted | | | |
| VAT on an import using postponed accounting | | | |
| Credit notes issued understated | | | |
| VAT on sales overstated | | | |

**38    JAYDEN**

Jayden is a VAT-registered trader making standard-rated supplies. He is unsure whether three purchase invoices he has received are correct and so has not yet processed them. If not, Jayden will ask the suppliers for a corrected invoice.

**(a)    Indicate whether each purchase invoice is correct or not.**

Tick one box on EACH line.

| | Correct | Incorrect |
|---|---|---|
| Invoice for purchase of a new car showing an amount exclusive of VAT of £10,000 and VAT of £2,000. The car is for use by an employee for business and private use. | | |
| Invoice for purchase of standard-rated services showing an amount exclusive of VAT of £3,000 and VAT of £3,600. | | |
| Invoice for purchase of reduced-rated goods showing an amount exclusive of VAT of £2,000 and VAT of £400. | | |

**(b)    Calculate the effect of processing each of the corrected invoices on the VAT payable by Jayden.**

Show increases as positive amounts and decreases as negative amounts.

| | Effect on VAT payable £0.00p |
|---|---|
| Invoice for purchase of new car | |
| Invoice for purchase of standard-rated services | |
| Invoice for purchase of reduced-rate goods | |

## 39 PRIYA

Priya makes taxable supplies. She has entered a purchase invoice into her VAT accounting software. The VAT calculated by the software (£108) does not agree to the VAT amount shown on the invoice (£90).

**(a)** **Indicate which one of the following is a possible reason for the difference.**

A    The supplier has offered a 20% prompt payment discount on a VAT-exclusive sale of £540.

B    The software has applied a standard rate of VAT to a reduced-rate supply of £648 inclusive of VAT.

C    Priya has entered the VAT-inclusive amount of £540 into the software as the VAT-exclusive amount.

D    The software has applied a standard rate of VAT to a zero-rated supply of £540 exclusive of VAT.

Conkatree Ltd offers a 7% prompt payment discount to customers who pay within 30 days of the invoice. The company issues sales invoices showing the full amount of the sale and VAT. A credit note is then issued if a customer pays in time to receive the discount.

Lewis purchased goods for £1,600 exclusive of standard-rated VAT and paid within 29 days. Conkatree Ltd has not yet raised the credit note.

**(b)** **(i)** **Calculate the VAT adjustment due to the discount.**

£

**(ii)** **Identify whether this adjustment increases or decreases the VAT payable by Conkatree Ltd.**

increases/decreases

## 40 MICK

Mick is responsible for submitting the VAT return for Otter Ltd, which makes taxable supplies. Mick understands how to treat sales and purchases in the UK, but Otter Ltd has started importing and exporting some goods.

Otter Ltd uses postponed accounting for import VAT and prepares and retains all relevant documents.

Mick wants help understanding the effect of this international trade on the input tax and output tax in the VAT return.

**(a)** **Complete the following statement.**

The effect on the VAT return of an import of goods is

A    an increase in input tax only

B    an increase in output tax only

C    no changes to either input tax or output tax

D    increases to both input tax and output tax

(b)   **Identify the output VAT to be included on the VAT return for an export of goods of £800 exclusive of VAT.**

A    £0

B    £40.00

C    £133.33

D    £160.00

## 41   BABATUNDE

Babatunde is an accounting technician for a company, which makes standard-rated supplies of services. Babatunde has entered a sale of £5,000 (exclusive of VAT) into the accounting software. The software shows output tax of £1,000 on the sale.

The company provides its services to customers in the UK and internationally. Babatunde is unclear about the customer for this sale and wants to know if the output tax calculated is correct.

(a)   **Indicate for which of the customers the VAT calculated by the software would be incorrect.**

Select ONE answer.

A    A business customer in the UK

B    A non-business customer in the UK

C    A business customer outside the UK

D    A non-business customer outside the UK

Babatunde realises that a credit note issued by a supplier in the last quarter had not been posted in the accounting software. The credit note showed a discount of £500 (exclusive of reduced-rate VAT).

(b)   **Identify the effect of the adjustment which must be made to reflect this.**

A    An increase in VAT payable of £25

B    An increase in VAT payable of £100

C    A decrease in VAT payable of £25

D    A decrease in VAT payable of £100

# VERIFYING VAT RETURNS

**Key answer tips**

Tasks will usually have two or three parts. Some of the questions in this section of the kit are multi-part whereas others give practice on the individual parts likely to be tested in this type of task.

These tasks cover some routine VAT calculations and reconciliations.

Topics include the treatment of errors, overseas transactions, and bad debts.

## 42 VAT ERRORS

(a) For each of the following businesses, indicate with a tick whether the non-deliberate error can be corrected on the next VAT return or whether separate disclosure is required.

|   | Net error £ | Turnover £ | Include in next return | Separate disclosure |
|---|---|---|---|---|
| 1 | 23,768 | 2,000,000 | | |
| 2 | 7,150 | 85,400 | | |
| 3 | 35,980 | 4,567,090 | | |
| 4 | 61,600 | 10,000,000 | | |

A business finds the following non-deliberate errors made in the previous quarter.

(i) VAT on a sales credit note has been recorded as £18 instead of £81.

(ii) VAT of £21.14 on a supplier invoice has been entered twice.

(b) **What is the net error?**

£ [            ]

**Will the error increase or reduce the VAT due on the next return?**

[ Increase/reduce ]

## 43 MURRAY LTD

At 31 March 2025, the VAT control account of Murray Ltd showed a balance due to HMRC of £4,937.50. The VAT return for the quarter to 31 March 2025 showed VAT due of £2,452.10.

(a) **Which of the following explains the difference?**

A   A VAT payment to HMRC of £2,485.40 has been included twice in the VAT control account.

B   Output tax of £2,485.40 has been included twice in the VAT control account.

Mel has written off a bad debt in his accounts. The amount was overdue by 10 months. The amount written off is £850 plus VAT of £170. Mel claims bad debt relief in his next VAT return.

(b) **Identify which statement correctly states the treatment of the bad debt in the VAT return.**

A   The amount in Box 1 is decreased by £170.

B   The amount in Box 4 is increased by £170.

C   The amount in Box 6 is decreased by £850.

D   The amount in Box 7 is increased by £850.

(c) **Identify which statement is incorrect in respect of the amount showing in Box 1 of a VAT return.**

A   The amount includes the value of cash sales inclusive of VAT.

B   The amount is reduced by VAT on prompt payment discounts taken up by customers.

C   The amount includes VAT fuel scale charges.

D   The amount includes VAT on imports under postponed accounting.

**44    DARCY**

At the end of the quarter, Darcy's VAT control account shows a balance due to HMRC of £3,946.82. The calculations for the VAT return show a balance due to HMRC of £3,814.32.

**(a)    Which of the following explains the difference?**

A    A bad debt (irrecoverable debt) of £795.00 (VAT-inclusive) which had previously been written off has now been recovered. The adjustment for this has been made in the VAT return calculations but not in the control account.

B    A credit note received on the last day of the quarter from a supplier, amounting to £662.50 excluding VAT, has been included in the VAT control account but not in the VAT return calculations.

Karl is an accounting technician who has recently been given responsibility for the VAT return. He looks at the previous VAT return to check he understands but discovers two errors in relation to credit notes.

(i)    VAT of £30 on a sales credit note has been treated as VAT on a sale.

(ii)    VAT of £45 on a supplier credit note has been entered twice.

**(b)    (i)    Identify whether each error affects input tax or output tax.**

Tick one box on each line.

| | Input tax | Output tax |
|---|---|---|
| VAT of £30 on the sales credit note | | |
| VAT of £45 on the supplier credit note | | |

**(ii)    Calculate the net error.**

£ 

**(iii)    Identify whether the net error has overstated or understated the VAT due.**

overstated/understated .

**45    BINGLEY**

At the end of the quarter, Bingley's VAT control account shows a balance of VAT recoverable from HMRC of £2,947.64.

After reviewing the records, the following items have been found which may affect the balance of VAT recoverable.

**(a)    Calculate the corrected figure of VAT recoverable after making the adjustments below:**

(i)    VAT of £237.00 on fuel scale charges has not yet been included.

(ii)    Bad debt relief on debts of £4,239.00 (VAT-inclusive) is to be claimed.

(iii)    An invoice for a lorry purchase of £20,000 excluding VAT has not yet been included.

£

Twigg Ltd makes wholly taxable supplies. Twigg Ltd's previous VAT return contains an error. The financial controller has asked Lauren, the accounting technician, to work out if the error can be corrected on the next VAT return.

Lauren looks at the amounts shown on the last VAT return.

|  | £ |
|---|---|
| Box 1 | 700,000.00 |
| Box 5 | 100,000.00 |
| Box 6 | 3,500,000.00 |

**(b)** **Identify the maximum error which could be corrected on the next VAT return. Choose ONE answer.**

A    £1,000

B    £10,000

C    £35,000

D    £50,000

Jim is a registered trader and makes a deliberate but not concealed error on his quarterly VAT return. The error understates VAT by £1,500.

**(c)** **Identify the correct statement regarding disclosure of the error to HMRC.**

A    The error must be disclosed to HMRC separately in writing or using form VAT652.

B    The error can be disclosed on the next VAT return, regardless of the level of Jim's taxable turnover.

C    The error can be disclosed on the next VAT return, provided Jim's taxable turnover exceeds £150,000.

D    No disclosure is required as the error is less than £625 per month.

## 46    ASHWIN

Ashwin has completed his VAT return for his latest quarter. It correctly shows VAT due to HMRC of £5,690.22.

The last quarter's VAT payment of £7,135.80 has been entered in the VAT account on the wrong side.

**(a)** **What is the <u>uncorrected</u> balance showing on the VAT account? Choose ONE answer.**

A    £12,826.02 VAT due to HMRC

B    £19,961.82 VAT due to HMRC

C    £1,445.58 due from HMRC

D    £8,581.38 due from HMRC

Toby voluntarily registered for VAT. He imports goods which would be standard rated if bought in the UK and has opted to use postponed VAT accounting.

All the goods he sells are standard-rated items.

In the quarter ended 31 December 2024 he makes export sales of £4,480 and imports of £4,000. Both these figures exclude VAT.

**(b)** **Indicate whether the following statements relating to the VAT return are true or false.**

Tick one box on EACH line.

|  | True | False |
|---|---|---|
| Box 1 includes output tax of £800.00 |  |  |
| Box 4 includes input tax of £800.00 |  |  |
| Box 6 includes the import of £4,000 |  |  |
| Box 7 includes the export of £4,480 |  |  |

## 47 REHMAN

Rehman has completed his VAT return for the last quarter. It correctly shows VAT due from HMRC of £1,768.50. The VAT account shows VAT due from HMRC of £2,488.00.

**(a)** **Which of the following explains the difference?**

A    VAT of £359.75 on purchase invoices has been posted on the wrong side of the VAT account.

B    VAT of £719.50 on purchase invoices has been posted on the wrong side of the VAT account.

C    VAT of £359.75 on sales invoices has been posted to the wrong side of the VAT account.

D    VAT of £719.50 on sales invoices has been posted to the wrong side of the VAT account.

Kevin is reviewing the draft VAT return of Lleaff Ltd prior to submission. This is the first quarter for which Lleaff Ltd will use the flat rate scheme. The relevant flat rate percentage (after reduction for the first year discount) is 12%.

Kevin reviews the amounts showing on the draft VAT return, which has been produced without taking account of the flat rate scheme.

|  | £ |
|---|---|
| Box 1 | 6,000.00 |
| Box 4 | 1,500.00 |
| Box 5 | 4,500.00 |
| Box 6 | 34,200.00 |
| Box 7 | 7,500.00 |

The total sales invoices and purchase invoices (inclusive of VAT where appropriate) that have been entered into the accounting software for the quarter are:

|  | £ |
|---|---|
| Sales invoices (standard-rated) | 36,000 |
| Sales invoices (zero-rated) | 4,200 |
| Purchase invoices (standard-rated) | 9,000 |

Kevin sees that the machinery cost account shows a single addition of £2,750 (exclusive of standard-rated VAT). The machinery purchase invoice is included in the amount of £9,000 above.

The VAT account shows an amount of £4,274.00 due at the end of the quarter. The previous quarter's liability was paid on time during the quarter.

**(a)** **Calculate the amount of output tax charged for the quarter under the flat rate scheme.**

£ [            ]

**(b)** **Calculate the amount of input tax which can be reclaimed for the quarter under the flat rate scheme.**

£ [            ]

**(c)** **Reconcile the VAT amount showing as due in the draft VAT return to the VAT payable figure per the VAT account.**

|                                          | £        |
|------------------------------------------|----------|
| VAT due in the draft VAT return          |          |
| Output tax overstated in the VAT return  |          |
| Input tax overstated in the VAT return   |          |
| VAT payable per VAT account              | 4,274.00 |

**48 HOLLY**

Holly runs a VAT-registered business. She discovers the following careless, non-deliberate errors in the recording of VAT on sales invoices in her records.

**(i)** VAT on an invoice to a customer recorded in June 2024 shows output tax of £297.55 when it should have been £279.55.

**(ii)** An invoice to another customer in July 2024 shows output tax of £480.00 when it should have been £840.00.

The VAT return for the 3 months to 30 November 2024 currently shows output tax of £3,556.40.

**(a)** **What would be the final figure for output tax on the VAT return for the quarter ended 30 November 2024?**

£ [            ]

Simon is a VAT-registered trader, making standard-rated supplies and purchases in the UK and internationally. When preparing his current VAT return, he realises he made two errors in the previous VAT return.

**(i)** An import was recorded correctly under postponed accounting, except that VAT of £306 was entered when the amount should have been £360.

**(ii)** The credit note from a UK supplier showed VAT of £228, when the amount should have been £288.

(b) **Identify the effect of correcting these errors on the VAT payable on the current VAT return.**

A    An increase in the VAT payable of £114.

B    An increase in the VAT payable of £60.

C    A decrease in the VAT payable of £6.

D    A decrease in the VAT payable of £60.

Daniel, an accounting technician, is reviewing a draft VAT return. He thinks there is an error in the return because the accounting software is not recognising a change in VAT legislation.

(c) **Identify which of the following actions would not be appropriate.**

A    Daniel asks his manager for her opinion on the issue.

B    Daniel checks with the software provider for any updates that may have been missed.

C    Daniel submits the VAT return as the software is more likely than him to be correct.

D    Daniel checks the GOV.UK website for information on the change concerned.

# RECORDKEEPING, FILING AND PAYMENT AND NON-COMPLIANCE

**Key answer tips**

Tasks in this area are likely to have more than one part. Some of the questions in this section of the kit are multi-part whereas others give practice on the individual parts likely to be tested in this type of task.

Areas assessed could include the rules regarding filing and payment of VAT returns and the impact of non-compliance with these rules, errors in VAT returns and HMRC's powers of assessment.

## 49 LO

**Lo has asked you to advise which of the following statements about records required for VAT purposes are true and which false.**

Tick one box on EACH line.

| | True | False |
|---|---|---|
| Businesses must keep records of all taxable and exempt supplies made in the course of business. | | |
| Taxpayers need permission from HMRC before they start keeping records electronically. | | |
| All vat-registered businesses must keep a VAT account. | | |
| The balance on the VAT account represents the VAT payable to HMRC or repayable by HMRC. | | |
| Sending or receiving invoices by electronic means is permitted but paper copies must also be kept. | | |
| Records should normally be kept for at least 3 years before being destroyed. | | |
| Failure to keep records can lead to a penalty. | | |

## 50 WYE LTD

Wye Ltd has not joined any of the special accounting schemes. It has annual taxable turnover of £100,000. Its quarterly return period ends on 31 July.

**(a)** **By what date should its VAT return be submitted?**

Select one answer.

A    31 August

B    6 September

C    7 September

D    None of the above

**(b)** **Identify which of the following statements about the retention of Wye Ltd's VAT records is incorrect.**

Select one answer.

A    Wye Ltd must keep VAT records digitally

B    The penalty for failure to keep records is £500

C    VAT records should be kept for six years

D    HMRC must be notified before Wye Ltd deletes any VAT records

**51 RAVI**

(a) **Ravi has asked you to advise him whether the following statements about businesses that have not joined any special accounting schemes are true or false.**

Tick one box for EACH line.

| | True | False |
|---|---|---|
| VAT is normally payable at the same time that the return is due. | | |
| Paying VAT by direct debit gives the business an extra 5 bank working days from the normal payment date before payment is taken from the account. | | |
| New businesses have a choice about whether they submit returns electronically or on paper. | | |
| Quarterly VAT returns are all made up to 30 April, 31 July, 31 October and 31 January. | | |

(b) **Identify which of the following traders would benefit from making monthly VAT returns.**

Select one answer.

A    Arthur makes wholly standard-rated supplies

B    Bert makes mainly standard-rated supplies but some exempt supplies

C    Clare makes mainly standard-rated supplies but some reduced-rated supplies

D    Darsh makes wholly zero-rated supplies

**52 VAT PENALTIES**

**Which of the statements are true and which false?**

Tick one box on EACH line.

| | True | False |
|---|---|---|
| A penalty can be charged if a trader fails to register at the correct time. | | |
| A registered trader who makes an error on a return leading to an underpayment of tax will always be charged a penalty. | | |
| If a registered trader does not submit a VAT return, then HMRC can issue an assessment to collect VAT due. | | |
| A penalty can be charged if a trader fails to notify a significant change in their types of supply to HMRC within 30 days. | | |

## 53    JAHEDA

Jaheda is a seamstress, she submitted her VAT return 10 days late, for the quarter ending 31 March 2025. All previous returns have been made on time.

**(a)    How much will Jaheda be charged for this late submission.**

| £ |
|---|

**(b)    Subsequently, Jaheda submitted her next 3 VAT returns late.**

**Tick one box for EACH line.**

|  | True | False |
|---|---|---|
| Jaheda will potentially receive a penalty point for each of her late submissions. |  |  |
| Jaheda will be charged £200 for each of her late submissions. |  |  |

## 54    LATE PAYMENT

Peter is a phone repairer; he paid his VAT 25 days late for quarter end 30 June 2025. The VAT due was £5,000. This was his first late payment.

**(a)    What will Peter have been charged for late payment for quarter end 30 June 2025 VAT return?**

| £ |
|---|

Murad buys and sells cars, he was late paying his VAT for quarter end 31 March 2025, payment of £3,400 was submitted 75 days late. This was the second time Murad was late paying his VAT.

**(b)    How much will Murad be charged for his late payment of VAT for quarter ended 31 March 2025?**

A    £152.77

B    £136.00

C    £27.95

D    £16.77

## 55    LUCINDA

Lucinda operates a VAT-registered business. She deliberately did not enter a standard-rated sale into her accounting software and has submitted the relevant VAT return. She has not concealed the error. HMRC have now discovered the error on the VAT return.

**(a)    Identify which of the following statements about a penalty due to the error is true.**

A    HMRC will not charge a penalty if this is Lucinda's first error

B    The maximum penalty is 100% of the VAT on the sale

C    The minimum penalty is 15% of the VAT on the sale

D    The maximum penalty is 70% of the VAT on the sale

William makes standard-rated supplies but failed to register for VAT when required on 1 August. William notified HMRC of this mistake and registered a month later on 1 September.

(b) **Identify which of the following statements about the late registration is true.**

   A    William must treat the sales in August as exempt supplies.

   B    If William's August customers refuse to pay extra to cover the VAT William should have charged, no VAT is due for the August sales.

   C    A penalty may not be charged if the late registration is non-deliberate.

   D    William had reasonable excuse for late registration if he did not know the VAT laws.

## 56    ERRORS AND OMISSIONS

(a) **For each of the following errors or omissions regarding VAT, insert in the table below the letter that explains the appropriate action from the list below.**

Appropriate actions:

   A    Trader must correct the error.

   B    HMRC can issue an assessment to collect tax due.

   C    HMRC can issue an assessment to collect tax due and charge a penalty.

   D    Trader must correct the error and HMRC can charge a penalty.

| Error/omissions | Action |
|---|---|
| Failing to register | |
| Failure to submit a return | |
| Making a careless or deliberate error | |
| Making a non-careless error | |

(b) **For each of the following errors or omissions regarding VAT, insert in the table below the letter that states the maximum penalty for that error or omission from the list below.**

Maximum penalty:

   A    30% of potential lost revenue

   B    70% of potential lost revenue

   C    100% of potential lost revenue

   D    £100

   E    £300

   F    £400

| Error/omissions | Maximum penalty |
|---|---|
| Making a deliberate and concealed error | |
| Failing to notify HMRC within 30 days that the HMRC assessment of VAT is too low | |

## PRINCIPLES OF PAYROLL

**Key answer tips**

Tasks in this area are likely to have more than one part. Some of the questions in this section of the kit are multi-part whereas others give practice on the individual parts likely to be tested in this type of task.

Areas assessed could include the employer's responsibilities of payroll or the operation of payroll.

**57  PETRA**

(a)  **Identify which one of the following scenarios does not require the individual to register as an employer.**

Select ONE answer.

A   Petra operates a market stall and takes on a part-time worker, paying a wage of £200 per week.

B   Steve hires a nanny to look after his children on weekdays.

C   Rhea starts a business, offering only her services as a tour guide.

D   Tamar runs a cleaning business with staff and her accountancy firm operates the payroll.

Susan started her business on 1 January. She employs her first employee Ricky from 1 August. Susan will pay Rick on the 28<sup>th</sup> of each month.

(b)  **Identify which one of the following statements about registering as an employer is true.**

Select ONE answer.

A   Susan can register from 1 January.

B   Susan must register by 1 January.

C   Susan must register by 1 August.

D   Susan must register by 28 August.

Employers deduct income tax (PAYE) and national insurance contributions from employees' salaries when paying those employees. These deductions are paid over to the relevant tax authority for payroll.

(c)  **Identify which one of the following organisations is the relevant tax authority for payroll.**

Select ONE answer.

A   The local council where the business is located

B   The Department for Work and Pensions

C   HMRC

D   AAT

58 **LEYLA**

Leyla wants help understanding the records she must keep for payroll purposes.

(a) **Identify whether each of the following statements is true or false.**

Tick one box for EACH line.

| | True | False |
|---|---|---|
| Failure to keep payroll records gives rise to a penalty of £500. | | |
| Employers must submit payroll information online to HMRC using HMRC's software Basic PAYE Tools. | | |
| Payroll records must be kept for three years. | | |

(b) **Identify which TWO of the following statements regarding a PAYE inspection (Employer Compliance Review) is not correct.**

Select TWO answers.

A    HMRC must have evidence that the employer has failed to comply with payroll legislation in order to visit the employer's business premises.

B    An employer who discloses errors in payroll filings to HMRC, during a payroll visit, is making a prompted disclosure.

C    If an error discovered during a visit from HMRC is deliberate but not concealed, the maximum penalty is 100% of the potential lost revenue due to the error.

D    An employer is usually given advanced notice of HMRC's visit and must give HMRC access to the payroll records during the visit.

59 **MAPPEL LTD**

Mappel Ltd provides taxable benefits to its employees.

(a) **Complete the following statements using the words on the right.**

Tick the appropriate column for each statement.

| | P11D | P60 |
|---|---|---|
| Mappel Ltd must complete a form .... to record an employee's benefits for a tax year. | | |

| | the employee only | HMRC only | both the employee and HMRC |
|---|---|---|---|
| This form must be given to .... | | | |

| | 31 May | 6 July |
|---|---|---|
| The employer must provide the form by ... following the end of the tax year. | | |

**(b)** **Identify the relevant data protection principle being applied in each of the following cases.**

Choose from the list of options below.

| | Principle |
|---|---|
| The payroll department only collects the information needed from an employee to operate payroll correctly. | |
| An employee's bank details are encrypted. | |
| An instruction on the employees' payslips requests employees check their personal details and inform the payroll department of any changes. | |

**Options:**

Lawfulness, fairness and transparency

Purpose limitation

Data minimisation

Accuracy

Storage limitation

Integrity and security (confidentiality)

Accountability

## 60 TOM

Tom earns a salary of £3,000 per month, but only receives £2,177.18 from his employer each month. He reviews his payslip for August which shows for the month:

| | £ |
|---|---|
| Salary | 3,000.00 |
| Deductions: | |
| Pension contributions to occupational pension scheme | (210.00) |
| | 2,790.00 |
| PAYE | (348.50) |
| Employee's NIC | (264.32) |
| Payment to employee | 2,177.18 |

**(a)** **Complete the table for each monthly amount by selecting figures from above.**

| | £0.00 |
|---|---|
| Gross pay | |
| Taxable pay | |
| Net pay | |

Sanjeev works in a restaurant and thinks his employer makes too many deductions before paying him each week. He wants help understanding the deductions.

**(b)    Identify whether the following statements are true or false.**

Tick one box for EACH line.

| | True | False |
|---|---|---|
| The employer must make deductions of PAYE and employee's NIC as these are statutory deductions. | | |
| The employer must deduct certain pension contributions unless Sanjeev has opted out of auto-enrolment. | | |
| Sanjeev can opt for his student loan to be repaid directly by deductions from his wages. | | |
| The restaurant may make deductions for breakages by Sanjeev, provided there is a prior written agreement for this in place. | | |

## 61    JOLENE

Jolene is the payroll assistant at Branch Ltd. There have been several employee changes and Jolene is unsure of the company's payroll obligations in respect of these.

**(a)    Identify TWO actions which Jolene must take when Amy starts work for Branch Ltd.**

Select TWO answers

A       Use Amy's P45 or new starter checklist to determine Amy's tax code.

B       Send a copy of Amy's P45 to HMRC before the first payment date.

C       Email Amy's P45 to Amy's line manager to introduce Amy.

D       Enter Amy's details on the Full Payment Submission (FPS) on Amy's first payday.

In May 2025, Jolene prepares the P60 forms for the tax year ending 5 April 2025.

**(b)    Identify whether a P60 form is required for each of the following employees.**

Tick one box for EACH line.

| | P60 required | Not required |
|---|---|---|
| Abe – employed throughout the tax year | | |
| Barbara – left Branch Ltd on 31 January 2025 | | |
| Careem – joined Branch Ltd on 1 February 2025 | | |
| David – left Branch Ltd on 30 April 2025 | | |

## 62  VIKRAM

Vikram is an accounting technician who has been given the responsibility for preparing the October 2024 payroll for the business. Employees are paid on 29 October 2024. All payments are made electronically.

(a)  **Identify the latest date by which the full payment submission (FPS) must be submitted to HMRC.**

Select ONE answer.

A    22 October 2024

B    29 October 2024

C    5 November 2024

D    22 November 2024

(b)  **Identify whether each of the following pieces of information is required on the full payment submission (FPS) for October 2024.**

Tick one box for EACH line.

|  | Required | Not required |
|---|---|---|
| Each employee's taxable pay and pay subject to national insurance contributions (NIC) for pay period |  |  |
| Each employee's PAYE and NIC deducted from the October payment |  |  |
| Employer's national insurance contributions for each employee |  |  |
| The leaving date for any employees if this is the FPS of their final payment |  |  |
| The starting dates of all employees working in the business |  |  |

## 63  ANTHONY

Anthony operates a small business but will not make any payments to employees this month.

(a)  **Identify which of the following reports Anthony should submit to HMRC in the month he makes no payments.**

Select ONE answer.

A    EPS (Employer Payment Summary)

B    FPS (Full Payment Submission)

C    P60

D    P45

Karen is late submitting her FPS (full payment submission) for the month and wants to know the consequences.

**(b)** **Identify whether each of the following statements about the penalty for the late FPS submission is true or is false.**

Tick one box for EACH line.

|  | True | False |
|---|---|---|
| The penalty depends on the number of employees of the business |  |  |
| The penalty is charged as a percentage of the deductions showing on the FPS |  |  |
| Karen will avoid a penalty if this is her first late submission in the tax year |  |  |
| If the FPS is submitted within three days of the due date, a penalty is only charged if Karen regularly submits the FPS late. |  |  |
| A further penalty is charged if the FPS is more than six months late |  |  |

**(c)** **Identify which of the following entries would not be found on an employee's form P45.**

Select ONE answer.

A   The employee's tax code at the leaving date

B   The tax deducted from the employee's pay from the start of the tax year to the leaving date

C   The employer's PAYE reference

D   The starting date of the employee's new employment

# REPORTING INFORMATION ON VAT AND PAYROLL

**Key answer tips**

This task assesses communication of information regarding VAT and payroll. This question is computer marked so will not be assessed by way of a free entry question.

Tasks are usually made up of a number of parts. This task in the practice assessments covered areas such as updates to software, special accounting schemes and when to use them, approval and submission of payroll information and sources of payroll information.

PRACTICE QUESTIONS: **SECTION 1**

## 64 BARCLAY

(a) **Barclay asks you why it is important to keep up-to-date with VAT rules. Which one of the following is NOT a good reason to keep up-to-date?**

Select ONE answer.

A    It helps you to ensure that the business avoids VAT penalties.

B    It is important for the ethical principle of professional competence to keep up-to-date.

C    It helps you to know when the business should register for VAT.

D    It helps you to know how the business may evade VAT.

Emma is an accounting technician. She wants to keep up-to-date with changes to VAT and payroll legislation and practice, but does not know where to find the information.

(b) **Identify which TWO of the following are appropriate sources of such information.**

Select TWO answers.

A    GOV.uk website

B    Comments section of a news website

C    A free online webinar given by HMRC

D    Social media

## 65 DHONI LTD

You are an accounting technician who has prepared the VAT return for Dhoni Ltd for the quarter ended 31 December 2024.

Today's date is 17 January 2025.

In the quarter ended 30 September 2024 output tax was understated by £4,672.90. The figure from Box 6 of the return for the quarter ended 31 December 2024 is £210,050.

**Complete the following email to the financial accountant explaining whether the error can be corrected on the VAT return to 31 December 2024.**

For words in bold, select the correct word/phrase.

| Email | |
|---|---|
| **To:** | Financial Accountant |
| **From:** | Accounting technician |
| **Date:** | 17 January 2025 |
| **Subject:** | VAT error |

An error occurred in the VAT return for the quarter ended 30 September 2024. Output tax of £4,672.90 was **(over/understated)**. This resulted in VAT being **(over/under paid)**.

This error **(was included on the VAT return to 31 December 2024/must be separately notified to HMRC)**.

Kind regards

KAPLAN PUBLISHING                                                                          45

**66    BELL**

You are an accounting technician working for a firm of accountants. You have just completed the VAT return for the quarter to 31 March 2025 for one of your clients, Andrew Bell.

Andrew Bell wrote off a debt of £6,467 on 28 February 2025. This debt had been outstanding since 15 August 2024.

**(a)    Complete the following email to Andrew Bell explaining how you have dealt with the irrecoverable (bad) debt.**

For words in bold, select the correct word/phrase. The date is 17 April 2025.

| Email |
|---|
| **To:**    Andrew Bell |
| **From:**    Accounting technician |
| **Date:**    17 April 2025 |
| **Subject:**    Irrecoverable (bad) debt relief |
| |
| Thank you for advising me about the debt you wrote off. I have included relief for this in the VAT return for the quarter ended (……………………………………………….). |
| Relief can be claimed because the debt was due for payment more than (**3 months/ 6 months**) ago. |
| The (**input/output**) tax paid on the original invoice can be reclaimed by including the amount in (**Box 1/Box 4**). The amount of irrecoverable (bad) debt relief is (£…………………). |
| Kind regards |

You are an accounting technician working for a firm of accountants. Your manager has suggested to Jessica, one of the firm's clients, that she should use the annual accounting scheme for VAT, adopting the monthly payment option. Jessica wants to understand what this means for the payment of VAT.

**(b)    Complete the following email to Jessica explaining the effect of adopting the annual accounting scheme on VAT payments.**

For words in bold, select the correct word/phrase. The date is 1 May 2024.

| Email |
|---|
| **To:**    Jessica |
| **From:**    Accounting technician |
| **Date:**    1 May 2024 |
| **Subject:**    Annual accounting scheme for VAT |
| |
| Under the annual accounting scheme you pay (**nine/ten**) monthly payments of VAT during the accounting period. The first payment is due at the end of (**month two/month four**) of the accounting period. Each monthly payment is (**10%/20%**) of the previous year's liability. |
| A balancing payment is due (**one month and seven days/two months**) after the end of the accounting period. |
| Kind regards |

## 67 SEABORN LTD

Seaborn Ltd is a new company that has just voluntarily registered for VAT.

Seaborn Ltd makes mainly standard-rated supplies with a few zero-rated supplies. It does not use any special accounting schemes.

You are an accounting technician. Today's date is 5 September 2024.

**(a)** **Complete the following email to the financial accountant advising generally when VAT returns must be filed.**

For words in bold, select the correct word/phrase.

| Email |
|---|
| **To:** Financial Accountant |
| **From:** Accounting Technician |
| **Date:** 5 September 2024 |
| **Subject:** Filing VAT returns |
| VAT returns must be submitted (**monthly/quarterly/yearly**) unless you are a net repayment trader when returns can be made (**monthly/quarterly/yearly**). |
| Returns must be filed within (**7 days/30 days/1 month and 7 days**) after the end of the VAT period. |
| You (**have a choice as to whether you file returns on paper or online/must file online**). |
| Kind regards |

Evan is the accounting technician at Trunck Ltd and is responsible for preparing the VAT return. Evan wants to impress the finance director Jodie so that he may get promoted.

**(b)** **Identify when Evan should submit each VAT return.**

Select ONE answer.

A    As soon as Evan has completed it, to avoid missing the filing deadline.

B    After ringing the HMRC helpline and discussing the amount payable.

C    Only when Trunck Ltd has sufficient funds to pay the VAT.

D    After Jodie has reviewed the return and authorised the submission.

**68 MILES LTD**

You are an accounts assistant working for Miles Ltd. From 1 September 2024 the company's main product is changing from being zero-rated to standard-rated.

**Complete the following email to be circulated to the Miles Ltd sales and sales invoicing staff.**

For words in bold, select the correct word/phrase. Today's date is 14 July 2024.

---

**Email**

**To:** All Sales and Sales Invoicing Staff

**From:** Accounts Assistant

**Date:** 14 July 2024

**Subject:** Change in VAT treatment

As you know the company's main product has been reclassified from one that is (**zero-rated/standard-rated**) to one that is (**zero-rated/standard-rated**).

All sales invoices (**issued on or after 1 September/with a tax point on or after 1 September**) must have the standard rate of VAT applied.

As we have decided to keep our VAT-inclusive prices the same, the price of goods to our customers will (**increase/decrease/stay the same**) and our profits will (**increase/decrease/ stay the same**).

Kind regards

---

**69 ELSIE**

You are employed by Elsie as an accounts assistant. Your supervisor is Abed.

You have only been working for a week and you are due to have training to learn how to deal with VAT accounting on areas that are completely new to you.

Unfortunately, Abed is very busy and has no time to train you before the VAT return is due.

Abed says 'This return is due in 2 days. Just guess the bits you are not sure about'.

**(a) Which of the following would be a suitable course of action?**

A   You are a bit nervous about bothering your supervisor so you do prepare the return and guess the bits you do not know.

B   You research the areas of which you are unsure. Although you are still not happy with all areas you go ahead and prepare the return.

C   You research the areas of which you are unsure and refer your remaining queries to Abed.

You work for an accountancy firm and are reviewing a bad debt claim for a client. You notice that one of the bad debts relates to the business of a friend of yours. You are concerned this means your friend's business is not performing well.

**(b)    Identify which of the following is an appropriate action.**

A    You ask your friend how her business is performing but cannot reveal why you are asking.

B    You tell your friend that her business has appeared on a bad debt claim.

C    You do not mention anything to your friend but tell your family that the business might not be viable.

D    You mention this to no one outside of the client or your firm.

**70    JEFF**

You work as a payroll assistant for Jeff. Jeff operates a business and pays his employees on the 25$^{th}$ of each month. You have prepared the payroll for 25 August 2024.

From the payroll software you obtain the following information for the August payroll:

|  | £ |
| --- | --- |
| PAYE | 621.50 |
| Employee's national insurance contributions | 462.96 |
| Employer's national insurance contributions | 557.52 |
| Student loan deductions | 114.86 |
| Employee's pension contributions | 187.50 |
| Employer's pension contributions | 500.00 |

**(a)    Calculate the amount payable to HMRC for the August payroll.**

£

**(b)    State the date by which Jeff must make the electronic payments to HMRC.**

Jeff is concerned about cash flow and wants to know the consequences if he makes the payment late by 10 days.

**(c)    Complete the following sentences advising Jeff of the consequences of late payment of the payroll amounts to HMRC.**

For words in bold, select the correct word/phrase.

If this is the first late payment for the tax year, there is **no penalty/a penalty of £100**.

If this is not the first late payment for the tax year, the penalty depends on the number of **employees/late payments in the tax year**.

**71   OLGA**

Olga is an accounting technician working in the internal finance department of a company. She prepared last year's P11D forms to record employee benefits and will do so again this year.

Olga does not know whether there have been any changes to the law in terms of which benefits to record on the P11Ds.

**(a)   Identify which TWO of the following actions are not appropriate for Olga to take.**

Select TWO answers

A   Unless Olga's manager gives different instructions, Olga should prepare the P11Ds on the same basis as last year for consistency.

B   Olga should delay running any updates issued by the company's software provider to reflect changes to the law, if this means employees have to pay more tax.

C   Olga should read the HMRC Employment Bulletins on the GOV.UK website for advice on completing the P11Ds.

D   Olga should ask her manager to review the P11Ds before she submits them to HMRC.

**(b)   Identify which TWO of the following actions would breach the data protection principles for payroll.**

Select TWO answers.

A   A finance director gives an officer of HMRC access to the company's payroll records during a PAYE inspection.

B   The payroll department of a large company deletes payroll records, when the records are both three years old and are no longer needed to process payroll.

C   The payroll assistant accidentally sends an employee's payslip to the email address of a colleague with a similar name.

D   An accounting technician struggles to complete the P11Ds by the deadline and so copies the information to her private laptop to work on at home.

# Section 2

# ANSWERS TO PRACTICE QUESTIONS

## VAT PRINCIPLES, REGISTRATION AND DEREGISTRATION AND SPECIAL SCHEMES

**Key answer tips**

The chief examiner has said in the past that the most common reason for being not yet competent in registration tasks was a lack of knowledge of the registration rules, particularly the 'future turnover' rule for registration.

Candidates need to look more carefully at the figures supplied in the task and remember that a business can voluntarily register at any time: they do not have to be close to the threshold in order to do so.

Some did not know that VAT is a tax which is only suffered by the unregistered end purchaser, mainly the public, because all other parties in the chain of events which take goods from manufacturers to final sale to consumers can claim back any VAT they have been charged along the way.

Another surprising area which has clearly been presenting problems is identifying the appropriate scheme for a business given specific information. Candidates should have enough time to access the right guidance in the reference material to look up the rules to answer such questions.

## 1 HUGH

(a) The answer is B.

Statement (i) is false as Hugh would have to be expecting taxable supplies of less than the deregistration threshold of £88,000 in the next 12 months to avoid having to register now.

Statement (ii) is true. Sales of capital assets are not included in the total of taxable supplies for registration purposes. Hence the business has made only £81,000 of relevant taxable supplies and as this is less than the registration threshold of £90,000, the business does not need to register.

Statement (iii) is true. Businesses must notify HMRC within 30 days of the end of the month in which the registration threshold is exceeded and will be registered from the first day of the month, which starts one month after exceeding the threshold.

Statement (iv) is largely correct but the business will be registered with effect from the **start** of the 30 day period, not the end.

**Key answer tips**

Make sure you read written questions like this thoroughly.

Part (iv) looks correct at first reading. You have to look at it carefully to notice the error.

(b)

|  | Yes | No |
|---|---|---|
| A business that is ceasing to trade. |  | ✓ |
| A continuing business that expects to make supplies of £88,000 in the next year of which one quarter will be exempt supplies. | ✓ |  |
| A business that expects to make taxable supplies of £89,000 in the next 12 months. |  | ✓ |
| A continuing business which has been making taxable supplies of £92,000 per year but which has now switched to making wholly exempt supplies of the same amount. |  | ✓ |

*Tutorial note*

*A business can deregister if they wish to, if it is expected taxable turnover for the next 12 months is below the deregistration threshold (currently £88,000).*

*A business which has ceased to trade or which switches to making wholly exempt supplies MUST deregister. They cannot deregister voluntarily.*

*In the example above, only the second business can deregister voluntarily. They are expecting to make taxable supplies in the next 12 months of £66,000 which is below the deregistration threshold.*

**Key answer tips**

Information about this topic is included in the reference material provided in the assessment, so you do not need to learn it.

However, you need to be familiar with its location and content – why not look at it now?

**2   JENKINS**

(a)   The answer is B.

Individuals have one registration covering all their sole trader businesses but not those they run in partnership with others.

The two partnerships must be separately registered.

This makes 3 registrations in total.

***Tutorial note***

*A sole trader has a single registration covering all the businesses they run as a sole trader. Therefore, it is the combined turnover of all their businesses that must be checked to see if it is over the registration threshold. In this case, Jenkins has £120,000 from his sole trader businesses and must register.*

*Separate partnerships, but with the same partners, must also have a single registration, so if Jenkins and only his wife ran another business in partnership, they would have to include that in their partnership registration.*

*A company is a separate legal person; therefore it requires a registration in its own name.*

(b)   The answer is C.

A business making taxable supplies below the registration threshold (whether or not they are making exempt supplies) is not required to register but may register voluntarily.

Zero-rated supplies are taxable supplies.

The other statements are true.

**3   NASSER**

(a)   Voluntary registration

| | Would not voluntarily register |
|---|---|
| It makes their goods more expensive for other VAT-registered businesses. | |
| It makes their goods more expensive for businesses that are not VAT-registered. | ✓ |
| It helps to avoid penalties for late registration. | |
| It increases the business burden of administration. | ✓ |

*Tutorial note*

*Voluntary registration is open to all businesses that make, or intend to make, taxable supplies.*

*Voluntary registration is useful because:*

1    *It avoids the possibility of penalties for late registration.*

2    *It disguises the small size of the business.*

3    *It is useful for businesses that sell zero-rated goods to register as they can still reclaim input tax (VAT on purchases).*

*Disadvantages of voluntary registration include:*

1    *It increases the burden of administration for small businesses.*

2    *It causes the sales price of goods to be increased by the addition of VAT. This is only a problem for those, like the public, who cannot recover VAT. Other VAT-registered businesses can recover the VAT so they would not be affected if the business voluntarily registered for VAT.*

*A person may consider not voluntarily registering if they will suffer the disadvantages above (i.e. increased administrative burden and if they have customers that are not VAT-registered).*

(b)    The answer is D.

**4    ISY**

(a)    The answer is C.

Taxable turnover is £8,200 per month and after 11 months, at the end of October, the business will have made £90,200 of taxable supplies.

*Tutorial note*

*The historic registration test is based on a business exceeding £90,000 of taxable turnover in the last 12 months or since starting in business if this is less than 12 months. Taxable turnover excludes exempt supplies but includes zero-rated supplies.*

**Key answer tips**

Information about this topic is included in the reference material provided in the assessment, so you do not need to learn it.

However, you need to be familiar with its location and content – why not look at it now?

(b)    The answer is YES.

## 5    DOOKU

| | Register now | Monitor and register later |
|---|---|---|
| A business with £50,000 of taxable turnover in the last 11 months but which expects taxable turnover of £92,000 in the next 30 days. | ✓ | |
| A business with taxable turnover of £5,000 per month for last 12 months. | | ✓ |
| A business with taxable turnover of £7,500 per month for the last 12 months. | ✓ | |
| A business with turnover of standard-rated supplies of £4,000 per month for the last year but which expects turnover of £50,000 in the next 30 days. | | ✓ |

*Tutorial note*

*Under the historic registration test a business must register if it has in excess of £90,000 of taxable turnover in the last 12 months or since starting in business if this is less than 12 months.*

*Under the future turnover test a business must register if taxable turnover of more than the registration threshold is expected in the next 30 days alone.*

*The first business has to register under the future test as they are expecting £92,000 of turnover in the next 30 days and the third business under the historic test (12 months × £7,950 = £95,400).*

## 6    CERTIFICATE OF REGISTRATION

(a)    The answer is C.

(b)    HMRC powers

| | Is a power | Is not a power |
|---|---|---|
| Charging penalties for breaches of VAT rules | ✓ | |
| Completing VAT returns | | ✓ |
| Inspecting premises | ✓ | |
| Providing suitable books for VAT record keeping | | ✓ |
| Changing the rate of VAT | | ✓ |

*Tutorial note*

*The certificate of registration proves that a business is registered for VAT. It shows the VAT registration number which must be shown on their invoices.*

*The rate of VAT is changed by legislative procedure, not unilaterally by HMRC.*

(c)    The answer is D.

Answer A is incorrect because HMRC is the relevant tax authority for VAT for the whole of the UK.

Answer B is incorrect as HMRC issues guidance concerning VAT law but Parliament is responsible for new legislation.

Answer C is incorrect as registered businesses pay the collected VAT over to HMRC.

**7    REMONA**

(a)    The answer is C.

A is incorrect. If the trader registers late, they will be liable to pay over the VAT for the period from which they should have registered to the date they did. However, the sales charged during this time will be treated as gross of VAT, so the VAT is calculated as £15,000 × 1/6 = £2,500.

B is incorrect, as the turnover for the historic test must be measured at the end of a month.

D is incorrect as some businesses (e.g. ones making zero-rated supplies) can have monthly returns and under the annual accounting scheme businesses just have one yearly return.

(b)

|  | True | False |
|---|---|---|
| Paper copies of electronic VAT records must be kept, in case of computer failure. | | ✓ |
| VAT records must be kept for six years. | ✓ | |
| A VAT-registered business must keep digital VAT records. | ✓ | |
| The maximum penalty for not keeping VAT records is 100% of the VAT due per the records. | | ✓ |

*Tutorial note*

*VAT records must be kept digitally to comply with Making Tax Digital (MTD).*

*The penalty for not keeping VAT records is £500.*

**Key answer tips**

Information about this topic is included in the reference material provided in the assessment, so you do not need to learn it.

However, you need to be familiar with its location and content – why not look at it now?

## 8    TROI

(a)    The answer is B.

**Working: Cumulative taxable turnover for the last 12 months**

|  |  | £ |
|---|---|---|
| End Dec 2024 | (£6,500 × 12) | 78,000 |
| End Jan 2025 | (£78,000 + £7,600 Jan 2025 – £6,500 Jan 2024) | 79,100 |
| End Feb 2025 | (£79,100 + £13,100 Feb 2025 – £6,500 Feb 2024) | 85,700 |
| End Mar 2025 | (£85,700 + £15,100 Mar 2025 – £6,500 Mar 2024) | 94,300 |

*Tutorial note*

*The historic registration test is based on a business exceeding £90,000 of taxable turnover in the last 12 months or since starting in business if this is less than 12 months. Taxable turnover excludes exempt supplies but includes zero-rated supplies.*

(b)    Answers A and D are correct.

B is incorrect as traders can only join the scheme if their annual taxable turnover does not exceed £1,350,000.  Once registered the trader must leave the scheme if their taxable turnover exceeds £1,600,000.

C is incorrect, as VAT invoices still have to be sent to customers.

## 9    ANNUAL ACCOUNTING

(a)    The answer is C.

(b)    The answer is B.

(c)    The answer is B.

(d)    The answer is B.

(e)    The answer is B.

**Key answer tips**

Information about this topic is included in the reference material provided in the assessment, so you do not need to learn it.

However, you need to be familiar with its location and content – why not look at it now?

*Tutorial note*

*The annual accounting scheme allows businesses to submit one VAT return each year. This is due two months after the year-end. No seven-day extension is allowed for electronic filing.*

*The scheme is not suitable for businesses that make zero-rated supplies. This is because such businesses can normally claim regular repayments of input tax, as they have no output tax to pay over. If they choose annual accounting, they will only get one repayment per year.*

*VAT payments on account have to be made throughout the year. VAT is not just paid once a year with the return. These payments on account are based on last year's VAT liability. If a business has a reducing turnover of taxable supplies, it will not benefit them to join the annual accounting scheme. This is because it will be making payments on account based on last year's higher VAT liability. If it used the normal accounting scheme, it would be paying lower VAT payments based on the current year's liability.*

*The trader must leave the scheme if the taxable turnover (excluding VAT) has exceeded £1,600,000.*

**10 ZED LTD**

    (a) The answer is C.

        Payments on account are 10% of last year's liability i.e. £7,290. Nine monthly payments are made at the end of months 4 to 12 in the accounting period.

    (b) The answer is D.

*Tutorial note*

*With the cash accounting scheme, the tax point date is the date the payment is received.*

## 11 TARAN

(a)

|  | True | False |
|---|---|---|
| Taxpayers must be up-to-date with their VAT returns before they are allowed to join the scheme. | ✓ | |
| Monthly payments on account are 10% of the previous year's VAT liability. | ✓ | |
| Monthly payments can be made using any method convenient to the taxpayer. | | ✓ |
| Monthly payments are made 7 days after the end of the month. | | ✓ |
| Monthly payments are made at the end of months 2 to 10 in the accounting period. | | ✓ |
| The scheme allows businesses to budget for their VAT payments more easily. | ✓ | |

**Tutorial note**

*Payments must be made electronically with no extra 7 days allowed.*

*Payments are made at the end of months 4 to 12 during the accounting period not 2 to 10.*

(b)     The answer is C.

VAT is calculated as 16.5% of £28,080 (£22,470 + £4,500 + £1,110) = £4,633.20.

The normal flat rate percentage must be replaced with 16.5% due to the business being a limited cost business.

## 12 FLAT RATE SCHEME

(a)

|  | Will benefit | Will not benefit |
|---|---|---|
| A business making solely zero-rated supplies to other businesses. | | ✓ |
| A business with a lower than average (for their trade sector) level of input tax. | ✓ | |
| A business with a higher proportion of standard-rated supplies than other businesses in the same trade sector. | ✓ | |

*Tutorial note*

*When using the flat rate scheme, businesses calculate how much VAT to pay over to HMRC by using a fixed percentage of their VAT-inclusive total turnover (including exempt supplies).*

*If a business makes wholly zero-rated supplies their output tax is £Nil and instead of having to pay VAT they can reclaim the input tax they have paid. With the flat rate scheme they would have to pay VAT instead of reclaiming it.*

*The flat rate percentage used by a business is fixed by reference to the average outputs less inputs for a typical business in that particular trade sector. If a business has lower than average inputs and hence input tax, they would benefit from using the flat rate scheme. Their overall VAT bill would be based on the higher trade sector proportion of inputs rather than their own lower figure.*

*The same logic would apply to the third business, which has a higher proportion of standard-rated supplies. The trade percentage used in the flat rate scheme would be based on a lower average of taxable outputs and hence should produce less tax than using normal VAT accounting.*

(b)     The answer is A.

Statements (i) and (iii) are reasons for using the annual accounting scheme. Statement (ii) is a reason for using the cash accounting scheme.

## 13   HACKETT

(a)     The answer is D.

The VAT is calculated on the total tax inclusive turnover. This involves taking the standard rated supplies (plus the VAT that will have been calculated on these) and the exempt supplies giving:

(£18,600 × 1.2) + £2,400 = £24,720.

If a business joins the flat rate scheme during its first year of VAT registration, a 1% discount on the usual flat rate percentage can be taken. This means the VAT is calculated as:

£24,720 × 10% = £2,472.00

(b)

|  | True | False |
|---|---|---|
| A business can join the flat rate scheme provided their taxable turnover for the next 12 months is expected to be less than £230,000. |  | ✓ |
| VAT due to HMRC is calculated as a fixed percentage of VAT-inclusive taxable turnover. |  | ✓ |
| VAT is shown on invoices calculated at the flat rate percentage. |  | ✓ |
| A business can be in both the flat rate scheme and the annual accounting scheme at the same time. | ✓ |  |
| The scheme cuts down on the time spent on VAT administration. | ✓ |  |
| Businesses cannot pay less VAT under the flat rate scheme than the normal method of accounting for VAT. |  | ✓ |

***Tutorial note***

*A business can join the flat rate scheme provided their taxable turnover (excluding VAT) is less than £150,000. They have to leave the scheme when their total turnover exceeds £230,000 (including VAT and exempt supplies.)*

*The VAT calculation is based on VAT-inclusive TOTAL turnover, not just taxable turnover.*

*VAT on invoices is calculated at the usual rate, not using the flat rate percentage.*

*It is possible for a business to pay less VAT under the flat rate scheme than under the normal accounting scheme.*

## CALCULATING AND ACCOUNTING FOR VAT

**Key answer tips**

The chief examiner has said in the past that the most common reason for being not yet competent in questions on these areas was as follows: poor skills in applying knowledge of tax points and the time limits for issuing VAT invoices.

Identifying the correct tax point is crucial to knowing the right VAT return on which to report inputs and outputs, and as such it is a critical area of compliance.

**14    CAIN**

    (a)    The answer is C.

    (b)    The answer is B.

    (c)    The answer is B.

*Tutorial note*

*The basic tax point is the date of delivery of goods or the date of performance of services. This is the case with (c).*

*However, if goods or services are paid for in advance or a tax invoice is issued in advance, the date of payment or the invoice date becomes the tax point date. This is the case with (b). The basic tax point is 24 August (i.e. date the goods are delivered). However, the actual tax point date is the date payment is received, as payment is received before the basic tax point date.*

*Where goods are not paid for or invoiced in advance, a later tax point can arise if a tax invoice is raised within 14 days after the basic tax point. This is the case with (a). This is referred to as the '14 day rule'. The basic tax point date is 15 May (i.e. date the goods are delivered). However, the actual tax point date is the invoice date as the valid invoice is issued and sent on 20 May (i.e. within 14 days of 15 May).*

**Key answer tips**

Information about this topic is included in the reference material provided in the assessment, so you do not need to learn it.

However, you need to be familiar with its location and content – why not look at it now?

**15   RATTAN**

(a)   The answer is B.

(b)   The answer is C.

(c)   The answer is A.

*Tutorial note*

*The basic tax point is the date of delivery of goods or the date of performance of services. This is the case with (a).*

*However, if goods or services are paid for in advance or a tax invoice is issued in advance, the date of payment or the invoice date becomes the tax point date. This is the case with (c). The tax point date in respect of the deposit is the date payment is received.*

*Where goods are not paid for or invoiced in advance, a later tax point can arise if a tax invoice is raised within 14 days after the basic tax point. This is the case with (b). This is referred to as the '14 day rule'.*

**Key answer tips**

Information about this topic is included in the reference material provided in the assessment, so you do not need to learn it.

However, you need to be familiar with its location and content – why not look at it now?

**16   ROGER**

(a)

| Deposit paid | Goods delivered | Invoice raised | Balance paid | Tax point for deposit | Tax point for balance |
|---|---|---|---|---|---|
| 10 March | 12 March | 30 March | 18 March | **10 March** | **12 March** (Delivery date) |
| 21 February | 7 March | 10 March | 1 April | **21 February** | **10 March** (14 day rule) |
| 13 May | 26 May | 11 June | 7 July | **13 May** | **26 May** (Delivery date) |

**Tutorial note**

*The basic tax point is the date of delivery of goods or the date of performance of services.*

*However, if goods or services are paid for in advance or a tax invoice is issued in advance, the date of payment or the invoice date becomes the tax point date.*

*If a part payment such as a deposit is paid in advance, then there will be two tax points, one for the deposit and one for the balance of the supply.*

*Where goods are not paid for or invoiced in advance, a later tax point can arise if a tax invoice is raised within 14 days after the basic tax point. This is referred to as the '14 day rule'.*

**Key answer tips**

Information about this topic is included in the reference material provided in the assessment, so you do not need to learn it.

However, you need to be familiar with its location and content – why not look at it now?

(b)

|  | True | False |
|---|---|---|
| A Proforma invoice is a valid tax invoice |  | ✓ |
| A customer receiving a pro-forma invoice can use it to reclaim the input tax shown. |  | ✓ |
| A modified invoice includes all the same details as a full invoice. |  | ✓ |
| Traders do not have to supply a VAT invoice unless their customer is VAT registered. | ✓ |  |

**Tutorial note**

*A pro-forma invoice is not a valid tax invoice, nor is it evidence that allows the customer to reclaim input tax.*

*Modified invoices also include the VAT inclusive amount for each product.*

*It is only compulsory to issue VAT invoices to registered traders.*

**17 BOLD**

(a) Zero-rated supply invoices

|  | True | False |
|---|---|---|
| The tax point date is 20 July. | ✓ | |
| The tax point date is 25 July. | | ✓ |
| An invoice for a wholly zero-rated supply is not a tax invoice. | ✓ | |
| Input tax recovery in respect of zero-rated supplies is restricted. | | ✓ |

*Tutorial note*

*An invoice for a wholly zero-rated supply within the UK is not a tax invoice. Hence, the 14-day rule cannot apply. The tax point date will be the earlier of the receipt of cash or the despatch of goods.*

*However, zero-rated supplies are taxable supplies and any input tax incurred in helping to make zero-rated goods or perform zero-rated services is fully recoverable.*

(b) The answer is C.

It is not a valid simplified invoice as the value of the supply exceeds £250. There is also no invoice number.

There is insufficient detail for it to be a valid full invoice.

**18 MARGARET**

(a) The answer is D.

A supplier credit note means a purchase credit note. VAT on purchase credit notes is deducted from input tax on purchase invoices so input tax will decrease. This would lead to an increase in the VAT payable for the period.

(b) The answer is B.

Exports to customers outside the UK are zero-rated provided there is evidence of export so there will be no effect on output or input tax.

## 19 MARGOT

|  | True | False |
|---|---|---|
| The receipt of a credit note from a supplier will reduce her output tax. |  | ✓ |
| The issue of a debit note to a supplier will reduce her input tax. | ✓ |  |
| The issue of a credit note to a customer will reduce her output tax. | ✓ |  |
| The receipt of a debit note from a customer will reduce her output tax. | ✓ |  |

*Tutorial note*

*Sales credit notes issued to customers are deducted from sales invoices and hence reduce the amount of output tax.*

*Purchase debit notes issued to suppliers are deducted from purchase invoices and hence reduce the amount of input tax.*

*A credit note from a supplier relates to purchases from that supplier. It is deducted from purchase invoices and hence reduces the amount of input tax.*

*A debit note from a customer relates to sales to that customer. It is deducted from sales invoices and hence reduces the amount of output tax.*

(b)    The answer is C.

(c)    The answer is D.

**Key answer tips**

Information about this topic is included in the reference material provided in the assessment, so you do not need to learn it.

However, you need to be familiar with its location and content – why not look at it now?

## 20   AHMED

(a)

|  | Required | Not required |
|---|:---:|:---:|
| Time of supply | ✓ | |
| Customer order number | | ✓ |
| Description of the type of supply | ✓ | |
| Rate of VAT applicable | ✓ | |
| General terms of trade | | ✓ |
| Total amount payable excluding VAT | ✓ | |
| Total amount of VAT payable | ✓ | |
| Acceptable methods of payment | | ✓ |

***Tutorial note***

*VAT invoices should contain the following:*

1   *Identifying number which must follow a sequence*

2   *Date of supply (or tax point) and the date of issue of the invoice*

3   *Supplier's name and address and registration number*

4   *Name and address of customer (i.e. the person to whom the goods or services are supplied)*

5   *Type of supply (e.g. sale, hire purchase, exchange etc.)*

6   *Description of the goods or service*

7   *Quantity of goods or extent of service for each separate description*

8   *Unit price, rate of tax and amount payable (in sterling) excluding VAT for each separate description*

9   *Rate of any discount offered*

10  *Total amount of VAT chargeable.*

*Simplified invoices need to show:*

1   *Identifying number which must follow a sequence*

2   *Date of supply*

3   *Supplier's name and address and registration number*

4   *Description of the goods or service*

5   *Rate of tax and amount payable (in sterling) including VAT for each separate rate of VAT.*

**Key answer tips**

Information about this topic is included in the reference material provided in the assessment, so you do not need to learn it.

However, you need to be familiar with its location and content – why not look at it now?

(b)     The answer is D.

(c)     The answer is B.

*Tutorial note*

*Sales credit notes are deducted from sales invoices and hence reduce the amount of output tax.*

*A supplier credit note is a purchase credit note. It is deducted from purchase invoices and hence reduces the amount of input tax. If input tax decreases, the amount of tax due to HMRC will increase.*

**21     EFFIE**

(a)     The answer is D.

(b)     The answer is B.

*Tutorial note*

*Retailers selling to the public do not need to issue a tax invoice to a customer unless they request one.*

*Any business can issue a simplified tax invoice provided the total amount (including VAT) does not exceed £250.*

*Retailers do not need to keep copies of simplified invoices. This is because retailers usually determine their VAT from sales records like till rolls rather than from a sales daybook listing of invoices.*

**Key answer tips**

Information about this topic is included in the reference material provided in the assessment, so you do not need to learn it.

However, you need to be familiar with its location and content – why not look at it now?

(c)    The answer is B.

**Tutorial note**

*For the purposes of the assessment, the basic tax point for goods on sale or return is the earlier of the:*

- *12 months from removal of the goods, or*
- *actual adoption of those goods.*

*The receipt of a payment for the goods is evidence that the customer has accepted the goods. Hence the customer has adopted the goods on 12 August.*

*An invoice is issued more than 14 days later; therefore the basic tax point is not overridden by the 14-day rule.*

## 22    SALLY

(a)

| | Can be issued | Cannot be issued |
|---|---|---|
| Standard-rated supplies of £210 | | ✓ |
| Standard-rated supplies of £170 plus zero-rated supplies of £40 | ✓ | |

**Tutorial note**

*A simplified invoice may be issued if the total of the invoice including VAT is £250 or less.*

*The first invoice will attract VAT of £42 (£210 × 20%) making a total of £252 which exceeds the limit.*

*The second invoice will attract VAT of £34 (£170 × 20%) making a total of £244 which is below the limit.*

(b)

| Item | Input tax recovered | Sale proceeds (excluding VAT) | Output tax |
|---|---|---|---|
| | | £ | £.pp |
| Computer | Yes | 400 | 80.00 |
| Car | Yes | 7,500 | 1,500.00 |
| Van | Yes | 6,100 | 1,220.00 |
| Car | No | 8,400 | Nil |

***Tutorial note***

*Output tax must be charged on the sale of capital assets, **except** for cars where no input tax was recovered.*

## 23 SCOTTY

(a) The answer is D.

***Tutorial note***

*The receipt of a refundable deposit does not create a tax point.*

*The basic tax point for goods on sale or return is the earlier of the:*

- *expiry of the fixed time period for adopting the goods (provided that is within 12 months), or*

- *actual adoption of those goods.*

*Here the basic tax point is 10 June as the goods are adopted before the fixed time period expires.*

*An invoice is issued within 14 days of the basic tax point; therefore the 14-day rule applies and the tax point becomes 21 June.*

**Key answer tips**

Information about this topic is included in the reference material provided in the assessment, so you do not need to learn it.

However, you need to be familiar with its location and content – why not look at it now?

(b) The answer is D.

|  | £ pp |
|---|---|
| AB Ltd (£562 × 20/120) | 93.66 |
| XY plc (£750 × 20%) | 150.00 |
| | ------- |
| Total output tax | 243.66 |
| | ------- |

**24   KIM**

(a)   The answer is B.

***Tutorial note***

*The basic tax point for services is when the service is performed. This is taken to be the date that all work has been completed except for invoicing.*

*In this case, the work is completed on 3 December so this is the basic tax point.*

*The invoice is issued more than 14 days later so the 14-day rule does not apply.*

**Key answer tips**

Information about this topic is included in the reference material provided in the assessment, so you do not need to learn it.

However, you need to be familiar with its location and content – why not look at it now?

(b)   The answer is D.

***Tutorial note***

*A modified invoice must include the VAT-inclusive and VAT-exclusive amounts, plus the amount of VAT.*

**Key answer tips**

Information about this topic is included in the reference material provided in the assessment, so you do not need to learn it.

However, you need to be familiar with its location and content – why not look at it now?

**25 BYRON**

(a)

| | True | False |
|---|---|---|
| If Byron invoices his customers on the last day of each month, then that day will be the tax point. | | ✓ |
| If Byron invoices his customers on the last day of each month, then the tax point will be the 20th of each month. | ✓ | |
| Byron can invoice his customers annually in advance, setting out the schedule of payments for the year. If he does this, his customers will be able to recover input tax for the year on receipt of that invoice, as the invoice date will be the tax point. | | ✓ |
| Byron can invoice his customers annually in advance, setting out the schedule of payments for the year. If he does this there will be twelve separate monthly tax points. | ✓ | |

*Tutorial note*

*The leasing of the plant and machinery is a continuous service.*

*The basic tax point is the earlier of:*

- *the date a VAT invoice is issued, or*
- *payment received.*

*In this case, the monthly direct debit is received before the VAT invoice is issued, so that fixes the tax point for each month.*

*However, when payments are received regularly a VAT invoice can be issued at the start of any period of up to one year (provided that more than one payment is due in the period) to cover all the payments due in that period.*

*For each payment the business should set out the following:*

- *VAT-exclusive amount*
- *date on which the payment is due*
- *rate of VAT*
- *VAT payable*

*In this case the business issuing the invoice does not have to pay all the VAT at the start of the year, but accounts for tax on the earlier of the:*

- *payment date for each regular payment, or*
- *date payment received*

*The customer can reclaim input tax at the same time.*

**Key answer tips**

Information about this topic is included in the reference material provided in the assessment, so you do not need to learn it.

However, you need to be familiar with its location and content – why not look at it now?

(b)    The answer is B

|  | £ |
|---|---|
| Reduced rate (£4,200 × 5/105) | 200.00 |
| Standard rate (£1,000 × 20%) | 200.00 |
| Total output tax | 400.00 |

# RECOVERY OF INPUT TAX

**Key answer tips**

The chief examiner has identified one problem area as the effect of the cash accounting scheme on bad debt relief.

Candidates need to remember that if a business uses the cash accounting scheme then the usual procedure for bad debt relief is irrelevant.

Candidates must read tasks very carefully to establish whether:

(a)    there is a bad (irrecoverable) debt, and

(b)    the business can claim bad (irrecoverable) debt relief on the VAT return.

If the task sets out that the business uses cash accounting then it has no opportunity, or need, to claim this relief.

**26    PUCK**

(a)    The answer is C.

*Tutorial note*

*For a partially-exempt trader, input tax suffered by a business has to be split between that relating to taxable and to exempt supplies.*

*Input tax suffered on goods and services used to create exempt supplies cannot normally be recovered. However, if the de minimis limits are not exceeded, all of the input tax can be recovered.*

*There are two parts to the test of whether the de minimis limits are exceeded. Here the portion of input tax relating to exempt supplies is less than 50% as required, but the amount of input tax relating to exempt supplies (£2,000) exceeds £625 per month. Therefore, only the input tax relating to the taxable supplies can be reclaimed.*

(b)    The answer is B.

Input tax can be reclaimed on the staff entertaining and the van.

Total supplies on which VAT can be recovered £10,040 (£890 + £9,150).

This is a VAT-inclusive total so the VAT included is £1,673.33 (£10,040 × 20/120).

**27    JERRY**

| | True | False |
|---|---|---|
| Traders who make only exempt supplies cannot register for VAT. | ✓ | |
| Traders who only make zero-rated supplies have to register for VAT. | | ✓ |
| Zero-rated supplies made by a registered trader are not classed as taxable supplies. | | ✓ |
| Traders making only exempt supplies cannot recover input tax. | ✓ | |
| VAT-registered traders making a mix of zero-rated and exempt supplies cannot recover any input tax. | | ✓ |

*Tutorial note*

*In order to register for VAT, a trader must be making or intending to make taxable supplies. Exempt supplies are not taxable supplies, so traders making only exempt supplies cannot register and cannot recover input tax.*

*Traders making only zero-rated supplies can register, as zero-rated supplies are taxable supplies. Such traders can also choose not to register if they wish to avoid the administration burden of dealing with VAT. However, they cannot reclaim input tax if they do not register.*

*Traders making a mix of zero-rated and exempt supplies can recover a proportion of their input tax. They can recover all their input tax provided that the input tax which relates to making exempt supplies does not exceed a 'de minimis' amount.*

## 28 DONNE

(a) The answer is D.

**Tutorial note**

*When a business makes both taxable and exempt supplies, it can normally only recover input tax relating to making taxable supplies plus a proportion of the input tax relating to overheads.*

*However, if the remaining input tax does not exceed a de minimis figure then all of the input tax can be recovered.*

(b)

| Description | Net £ | VAT £ | Gross £ | Reclaim input tax? |
|---|---|---|---|---|
| Repairs to machinery | 1,900.00 | 380.00 | 2,280.00 | **Yes** |
| Delivery van | 10,000.00 | 2,000.00 | 12,000.00 | **Yes** |
| UK customer entertaining | 640.00 | 128.00 | 768.00 | **No** |
| Overseas customer entertaining | 310.00 | 62.00 | 372.00 | **Yes** |
| Car (pool car with no private use) | 8,400.00 | 1,680.00 | 10,080.00 | **Yes** |

**Key answer tips**

Information about this topic is included in the reference material provided in the assessment, so you do not need to learn it.

However, you need to be familiar with its location and content – why not look at it now?

**Tutorial note**

*VAT cannot be recovered on entertaining, except for staff entertaining and entertaining overseas customers.*

*VAT cannot be recovered on the purchase of cars that have an element of private use.*

*Input tax can be recovered on cars which are 100% used for the business, such as pool cars.*

**29    SELDON**

(a)    The answers are A and C.

Answer A is wrong because the debt must simply have been written off. There is no time limit.

Answer C is wrong. There is no requirement that the customer should be formally insolvent, in administration or in liquidation.

Answers B and D are valid requirements.

**Key answer tips**

Information about this topic is included in the reference material provided in the assessment, so you do not need to learn it.

However, you need to be familiar with its location and content – why not look at it now?

(b)    The answer is D.

Both standard-rated and zero-rated supplies are taxable supplies. If no exempt supplies are made then the business can recover all their input tax.

(c)    The answer is C.

|  | £ |
|---|---|
| Output tax on scale charge (£368 × 20/120) | 61.33 |
| Input tax on petrol (£823.50 × 20/120) | (137.25) |
| Net input tax recoverable | 75.92 |

*Tutorial note*

*When a business provides private fuel for an employee, a VAT scale charge depending on the $CO_2$ emission level of the car is added to outputs and output tax is increased.*

*Input tax on all the fuel paid for by the business can then be recovered.*

*If you are provided with the $CO_2$ emissions of the car the relevant scale charge can be found in the reference material.*

**30    RAFA AND CO**

(a)    The answer is D.

Options A, B and C mean that the business is only claiming business VAT so there is no need to account for a fuel scale charge.

*Tutorial note*

*If a business does not want to pay a fuel scale charge it can do one of the following:*

(a)    *Reclaim only VAT on business fuel (detailed records of business and private mileage needs to be kept proving the business mileage), or*

(b)    *Not claim any VAT on fuel at all even for commercial vehicles. This has the advantage of being simple and is useful if mileage is low.*

(c)    *Only use fuel for business purposes.*

**Key answer tips**

Information about this topic is included in the reference material provided in the assessment, so you do not need to learn it.

However, you need to be familiar with its location and content – why not look at it now?

(b)    The answer is C.

Input tax can be recovered on half of the entertaining costs that relate to staff and on the van. No input tax can be recovered on entertaining UK customers.

(£10,700 + (50% × £780)) × 1/6 = £1,848.33

**31    VICTORIA LTD**

(a)    The answer is A.

$£263 \times 1/6 = £43.83$

*Tutorial note*

*When a business provides private fuel for an employee, a VAT scale charge depending on the $CO_2$ emission level of the car is added to outputs and output tax is increased.*

*The VAT fuel scale charge figure given in the reference material is the gross consideration (i.e. stated inclusive of VAT), so the VAT is found by multiplying by 1/6.*

**Key answer tips**

Information about this topic is included in the reference material provided in the assessment, so you do not need to learn it.

However, you need to be familiar with its location and content – why not look at it now?

(b)    The answer is A.

*Tutorial note*

*A business can reclaim the VAT according to the tax point of the purchase, which is not necessarily the payment date. This is usually the date the goods/services are made available to the customer or when the invoice is issued (if that is within 14 days of delivery).*

**Key answer tips**

Information about this topic is included in the reference material provided in the assessment, so you do not need to learn it.

However, you need to be familiar with its location and content – why not look at it now?

**32    MELINDA**

(a)

|  | Recover | Cannot recover |
|---|---|---|
| Purchases for resale | ✓ | |
| New laptop computer for Melinda's daughter | | ✓ |
| New desk for the business office (Melinda has lost the VAT receipt) | | ✓ |
| Motorcycle for business deliveries | ✓ | |

**Tutorial note**

*In order to claim back input tax on goods or services, the trader must have a valid VAT invoice and the items must be for business use.*

(b)    The answer is D.

|  | £ |
|---|---|
| Value of supply | 900.00 |
| Less: Bulk buy discount (£900 × 2%) | (18.00) |
| | 882.00 |
| Less: Prompt payment discount (£882 × 5%) | (44.10) |
| Amount for calculation of VAT | 837.90 |
| VAT at 20% | 167.58 |

Alternatively, this could be calculated as (£900 × 98% × 95% × 20%)

**Tutorial note**

*VAT must be accounted for on the amount that the customer actually pays.*

**33    LARISSA**

(a)    The answer is B.

| | £ |
|---|---:|
| Value of supply | 750.00 |
| Less: Prompt payment discount (£750 × 3%) | (22.50) |
| Amount for calculation of VAT | 727.50 |
| VAT at 20% | 145.50 |

Alternatively this could be calculated as (£750 × 97% × 20%)

(b)    The answer is D.

| | £ |
|---|---:|
| Discount (3% × £750.00) | 22.50 |
| VAT at 20% | 4.50 |
| | 27.00 |

**34    TRINA**

(a)    The answer is B.

VAT is £40.00 (£240.00 × 20/120)

**Tutorial note**

*An offer to pay a customer's VAT is simply a form of discount. If the customer pays £240.00, this will be treated as the VAT-inclusive sale proceeds.*

(b)    The answer is C.

**Tutorial note**

*A VAT invoice must be issued within 30 days of the earlier of the date of supply or the date of payment.*

# PREPARING, CALCULATING AND ADJUSTING INFORMATION FOR VAT RETURNS

**Key answer tips**

The chief examiner has said in the past that the most common reasons for being not yet competent in tasks on these areas were: dealing with errors, the effect on VAT of deposits paid, and the charging of VAT on sales abroad.

Too many candidates failed to understand the implications of deposits paid by a customer, and how this payment automatically creates a tax point for VAT and hence a reportable transaction.

## 35    KEIKO LTD

The VAT due is £2,076.66

|  | £ |
|---|---|
| Cash sales receipts | 780 |
| Receipts from customers | 39,745 |
|  | 40,525 |
| Less:  Cash paid to suppliers | (27,890) |
| Petty cash purchases | (175) |
| Net cash receipts | 12,460 |
|  |  |
| VAT at 20/120 | 2,076.66 |

*Tutorial note*

*When a business uses cash accounting, the relevant figures for VAT are taken from cash receipts and payments rather than from invoiced amounts.*

*Cash receipts and payments made will be the VAT-inclusive amounts.*

*Note that the layout above is not intended to represent a VAT account or VAT return. It is just a working to calculate VAT due.*

## 36    JULIE

The answer is B.

Output tax should be charged on the standard-rated sales and on the sale of plant.

Output tax is £9,029.00 ((£40,145 + £5,000) × 20%).

**37    AMANDA**

| | Increases balance payable to HMRC | Decreases balance payable to HMRC | No effect on balance payable to HMRC |
|---|:---:|:---:|:---:|
| VAT on purchases is understated | | ✓ | |
| Bad debt relief claim omitted | | ✓ | |
| Previous net over claim to be adjusted for on the next VAT return has been omitted | ✓ | | |
| VAT on an import using postponed accounting | | | ✓ |
| Credit notes issued understated | | ✓ | |
| VAT on sales overstated | | ✓ | |

*Tutorial note*

*A version of the VAT account as suggested in the VAT Guide is shown below.*

*If an entry is made on the debit side (left hand side) of the VAT account, it reduces the amount payable to HMRC.*

*If an entry is made on the credit side (right hand side) of the VAT account, it increases the amount payable to HMRC.*

*VAT on imports where postponed accounting is used is entered on both sides of the VAT account and therefore has no effect on the balance payable to HMRC.*

*If credit notes issued are understated, the amendment will decrease the VAT payable.*

**VAT account**

| VAT deductible – input tax | | VAT payable – output tax | |
|---|:---:|---|:---:|
| | £ | | £ |
| VAT suffered on purchases (1) | X | VAT charged on sales | X |
| VAT suffered on imports (4) | X | VAT charged on imports under postponed accounting (4) | X |
| | | | |
| Adjustments of previous errors (if within error limit) (3) | | | |
| Net input tax adjustment | (X) | Net output tax adjustment (6) | (X) |
| | | | |
| Bad debt (irrecoverable debt) relief (2) | X | | |
| | | | |
| Less: VAT on credit notes received | (X) | Less: VAT on credit notes allowed to customers (5) | (X) |
| | ___ | | ___ |
| Total tax deductible | X | Total tax payable | X |
| | ___ | | |
| | | Total tax deductible | (X) |
| | | | |
| | | Payable to HMRC | X |
| | | | ___ |

**38    JAYDEN**

(a)

| | Correct | Incorrect |
|---|---|---|
| Invoice for purchase of a new car showing an amount exclusive of VAT of £10,000 and VAT of £2,000. The car is for use by an employee for business and private use. | ✓ | |
| Invoice for purchase of standard-rated services showing an amount exclusive of VAT of £3,000 and VAT of £3,600. | | ✓ |
| Invoice for purchase of reduced-rate goods showing an amount exclusive of VAT of £2,000 and VAT of £400. | | ✓ |

(b)

| | Effect on VAT payable £ |
|---|---|
| Purchase of the new car | 0.00 |
| Purchase of standard-rated services | (600.00) |
| Purchase of reduced-rate goods | (100.00) |

*Tutorial note*

*The purchase of a new car will include VAT but this is not recoverable if there is private use the purchaser. Therefore, processing the invoice will have no effect on VAT payable.*

*The invoice for the standard-rated services is incorrect because the amount shown for VAT is the gross amount of the invoice including VAT.*

*The invoice for the reduced-rate goods is incorrect, as standard-rated VAT has been charged. The VAT should be £2,000 × 5% = £100.*

**39    PRIYA**

(a)    The answer is C.

A VAT-inclusive amount of £540 would include VAT of £540 × 1/6 = £90. This is the amount shown on the invoice. If Priya had entered £540 as the VAT-exclusive amount, the software would calculate VAT of £540 × 20% = £108.

Answer A is incorrect as the VAT on a sale of £540 after a 20% prompt payment discount is £540 × 20% × 80% = £86.40, and not £90.

Answer B is incorrect. If a sale of £648 (VAT-inclusive) is treated as a standard-rated supply then the VAT would be calculated by the software as £648 × 1/6 = £108. However, if this were a reduced rate supply, the VAT on the invoice would be shown as £648 × 1/21 = £30.85.

Answer D is incorrect. If a sale of £540 (VAT-exclusive) were treated as standard-rated, then the VAT would be calculated by the software as £540 × 20% = £108, but the invoice would show VAT of £0.

(b)   (i)   The VAT adjustment due to the discount is £22.40 (£1,600 × 20% × 7%).

       (ii)   This adjustment decreases the VAT payable by Conkatree Ltd.

## 40   MICK

(a)   The answer is D.

Otter Ltd uses postponed accounting and so must include the import tax and the output tax on the return. The company makes taxable supplies and recovers the equivalent input tax on the same return.

(b)   The answer is A.

Exports of goods are zero-rated, provided there is evidence of the export.

## 41   BABATUNDE

(a)   The answer is C.

A supply of a service to a business customer outside the UK (B2B) is treated as made where the customer is based, so there is no UK VAT charged. Supplies to UK customers and to non-business customers outside the UK are usual standard-rated supplies.

**Key answer tips**

Information about this topic is included in the reference material provided in the assessment, so you do not need to learn it.

However, you need to be familiar with its location and content – why not look at it now?

(b)   The answer is A.

The amount of VAT on the adjustment is £500 × 5% = £25. Too much Input tax has been recovered, and so the VAT payable will increase by the adjustment.

# VERIFYING VAT RETURNS

**Key answer tips**

The chief examiner has said in the past that the most common reason, by a significant margin, for being not yet competent in tasks on these areas is a problem in identifying errors that cause a discrepancy between the VAT account and the VAT return.

When the task sets out a failure to reconcile the VAT account and the VAT return, candidates need to take a step-by-step approach to the information provided. In most of these tasks there are two corrections to take into consideration. Candidates need to read the information given carefully and to practice this area more.

Other common mistakes regarding dealing with errors and omissions:

1    Failure to understand the error reporting threshold for separate notifications.

2    Belief that if a transaction was omitted from a previous return, it could be ignored – but omissions are errors and therefore action must be taken.

3    Not realising that a deliberate error is reportable, no matter what its value.

## 42    VAT ERRORS

(a)

|   | Net error £ | Turnover £ | Include in next return | Separate disclosure |
|---|---|---|---|---|
| 1 | 23,768 | 2,000,000 |  | ✓ |
| 2 | 7,150 | 85,400 | ✓ |  |
| 3 | 35,980 | 4,567,090 | ✓ |  |
| 4 | 61,600 | 10,000,000 |  | ✓ |

*Tutorial note*

*When a trader discovers a VAT error, they must inform HMRC. If the net error is less than a certain threshold and is not deliberate, it can be included on the next VAT return. If not, it must be disclosed separately on Form VAT 652 or in a letter.*

*The threshold operates as follows:*

*Net errors up to £10,000 can always be included on the next VAT return.*

*Net errors above £50,000 must always be separately disclosed.*

*Errors between these thresholds can be included on the next VAT return if they are no more than 1% of turnover (specifically the figure in Box 6 of the return).*

(b)     The net error is £41.86.

|  | £ |
|---|---|
| Output tax reduced by (£81 – £18) | 63.00 |
| Input tax reduced by | (21.14) |
|  | 41.86 |

This will reduce the VAT due.

## 43   MURRAY LTD

(a)     The answer is B.

The VAT due in the VAT control account is £2,485.40 too high.

This will occur if there are either too few debits or too many credits. Answer A would result in too many debits and hence a lower balance in the control account.

(b)     The answer is B.

Bad debt relief is claimed by including the VAT amount in Box 4. The output tax, sales and purchases amounts remain unchanged.

(c)     The answer is A.

Only the output tax on the cash sales, not the full VAT-inclusive amount, is included in Box 1.

The fuel scale charge is an amount of output tax. VAT imports accounted for under postponed accounting must be included as output tax (although the input tax may be recoverable under usual rules). Where customers have paid in time for prompt payment discounts to apply, the VAT on the discounted element is no longer included as output tax.

## 44   DARCY

(a)     The answer is B.

The VAT control account balance shows £132.50 more due to HMRC than the VAT return calculations.

VAT on the bad debt recovered is £132.50 (£795 × 1/6). This would increase the output tax to be shown in the control account and would increase the balance of VAT due. This cannot explain the difference.

The credit note received from a supplier (a purchase credit note) also increases tax due to HMRC by £132.50 (£662.50 × 20%). This needs to be included in the VAT return calculations and will increase the VAT due to HMRC.

(b)     (i)

|  | Input tax | Output tax |
|---|---|---|
| VAT of £30 on the sales credit note |  | ✓ |
| VAT of £45 on the supplier credit note | ✓ |  |

(b) (ii) The net error is £105.00.

| | £ |
|---|---|
| Output tax overstated by £30 × 2 | 60.00 |
| Input tax understated by | 45.00 |
| | 105.00 |

(b) (iii) The net error has overstated the VAT due.

## 45 BINGLEY

(a) The revised figure of VAT recoverable is £7,417.14

| | £ |
|---|---|
| Original VAT recoverable | 2,947.64 |
| Less: VAT due on fuel scale charges | (237.00) |
| Add: Bad debt (irrecoverable debt) relief (£4,239.00 × 1/6) | 706.50 |
| VAT recoverable on lorry purchase (£20,000 × 20%) | 4,000.00 |
| Revised figure of VAT recoverable | 7,417.14 |

(b) The answer is C.

Box 6 gives the taxable turnover for the return period. An error can be corrected on the next VAT return if it is lower than the greater of £10,000 and 1% of taxable turnover i.e. £35,000.

(c) The answer is A.

A deliberate error cannot be disclosed on the next VAT return, however small.

The de minimis limit of £625 per month relates to the partial exemption rules and not errors.

## 46 ASHWIN

(a) The answer is B.

A VAT payment should be debited to the VAT account but it has been credited in error. This means that the account is showing too many credits.

The credit side is £14,271.60 (2 × £7,135.80) too high and the uncorrected balance must be £19,961.82 (£5,690.22 + £14,271.60).

(b)

| | True | False |
|---|---|---|
| Box 1 includes output tax of £800.00 | ✓ | |
| Box 4 includes input tax of £800.00 | ✓ | |
| Box 6 includes the import of £4,000 | | ✓ |
| Box 7 includes the export of £4,480 | | ✓ |

**Tutorial note**

*Postponed accounting means Toby includes the output tax (Box 1) but can reclaim the input tax (Box 4).*

*Exports are zero-rated and therefore there is no VAT to include in box 1.*

*He includes the value of the import with other purchases in Box 7.*

*He includes the value of the export with other sales in Box 6.*

47  **REHMAN**

(a)  The answer is C.

The VAT account is showing a debit balance that is too high by £719.50 indicating that too many debits have been posted.

VAT on sales invoices should be credited to the VAT account so if posted on the wrong side (i.e. debit), this would explain the difference.

The amount posted on the wrong side is half of the error in the balance (i.e. half of £719.50, which is £359.75).

(b)  The amount of output tax charged under the flat rate scheme is £4,824 (12% × (£36,000 + £4,200)).

The amount of input tax claimed under the flat rate scheme is £550 (£2,750 × 20%).

|  | £ |
|---|---|
| VAT due in the draft VAT return | 4,500.00 |
| Output tax overstated in the VAT return | (1,176.00) |
| Input tax overstated in the VAT return | 950.00 |
| VAT payable per VAT account | 4,274.00 |

The output tax overstated = £6,000.00 – £4,824.00 = £1,176.00

The input tax overstated = £1,500 – £550 = £950

**Tutorial note**

*When the flat rate scheme is used, the output VAT in the return is that given by applying the flat rate percentage to the total VAT-inclusive sales.*

*Input VAT is not reclaimed, except for that on capital assets costing at least £2,000.*

**48    HOLLY**

(a)    The final figure of output tax will be £3,898.40.

|  |  | £ |
|---|---|---|
| Original output VAT figure | | 3,556.40 |
| Less: VAT overstated (£297.55 – £279.55) | | (18.00) |
| | | 3,538.40 |
| Add: VAT understated (£840.00 – £480.00) | | 360.00 |
| Revised output VAT figure | | 3,898.40 |

(b)    The answer is B.

The VAT on the credit note from the supplier should be £60 greater, reducing input tax by £60 and so increasing the VAT payable by £60.

An error in the recording of the VAT amount on an import will have no overall effect on the VAT payable as the output tax and input tax should be changed by the same amount.

*Tutorial note*

*Postponed accounting of an import means the trader recognises output VAT on the import. However, if the trader makes wholly taxable supplies, the same amount of input VAT can be recovered.*

(c)    The answer is C.

If in doubt, a line manager should be consulted. Software updates may take some time to reflect legislative changes, and the updates must be installed to take effect.

# RECORDKEEPING, FILING AND PAYMENT AND NON-COMPLIANCE

**49    LO**

| | True | False |
|---|---|---|
| Businesses must keep records of all taxable and exempt supplies made in the course of business. | ✓ | |
| Taxpayers need permission from HMRC before they start keeping records electronically. | | ✓ |
| All businesses must keep a VAT account. | ✓ | |
| The balance on the VAT account represents the VAT payable to HMRC or repayable by HMRC. | ✓ | |
| Sending or receiving invoices by electronic means is permitted but paper copies must also be kept. | | ✓ |
| Records should normally be kept for at least 3 years before being destroyed. | | ✓ |
| Failure to keep records can lead to a penalty. | ✓ | |

**Tutorial note**

*VAT records should be kept for 6 years. They must be kept in electronic format and should be easily accessible to HMRC during an enquiry (there is no need for them to be kept at the business's registered office). Records include purchases, purchase returns day book, sales, sales returns day book, cashbook, invoices, credit notes, delivery notes, bank statements and the VAT summary (ledger account).*

**50    WYE LTD**

(a)    The answer is C.

**Tutorial note**

*When a business makes a VAT return it has one month and 7 days from the end of the VAT period to submit the return online.*

(b)    The answer is D.

**Tutorial note**

*It is mandatory for VAT registered businesses to keep digital records and submit VAT returns online under the Making Tax Digital regime.*

*VAT records can be deleted once the statutory retention period of six years has passed.*

**51 RAVI**

(a)

| | True | False |
|---|---|---|
| VAT is normally payable at the same time that the return is due. | ✓ | |
| Paying VAT by direct debit gives the business an extra 5 bank working days from the normal payment date before payment is taken from the account. | | ✓ |
| New businesses have a choice about whether they submit returns electronically or on paper. | | ✓ |
| Quarterly VAT returns are all made up to 30 April, 31 July, 31 October and 31 January. | | ✓ |

*Tutorial note*

*VAT payments are due at the same time as the return. Funds must clear HMRC bank account within 1 month and 7 days of the end of the VAT return period.*

*Direct debit payments are taken from the business bank account 3 bank working days from the normal payment date.*

*All new businesses have to use electronic returns. There is no choice.*

*There are three sets of quarterly return dates, not one. HMRC allocate businesses to one of the sets of dates to spread out the flow of returns submitted.*

**Key answer tips**

Information about this topic is included in the reference material provided in the assessment, so you do not need to learn it.

However, you need to be familiar with its location and content – why not look at it now?

(b) The answer is D.

*Tutorial note*

*A trader making wholly zero-rated supplies has no output tax but can reclaim input tax, and so is due a refund each VAT period. By choosing to make monthly returns, the trader can receive these repayments more quickly which improves cash flow.*

## 52 VAT PENALTIES

|  | True | False |
|---|---|---|
| A penalty can be charged if a trader fails to register at the correct time. | ✓ | |
| A registered trader who makes an error on a return leading to underpayment of tax will always be charged a penalty. | | ✓ |
| If a registered trader does not submit a VAT return, then HMRC can issue an assessment to collect VAT due. | ✓ | |
| A penalty can be charged if a trader fails to notify a significant change in their types of supply to HMRC within 30 days. | ✓ | |

*Tutorial note*

*A penalty can be charged if a business does not register on time.*

*If an error is neither careless nor deliberate and the trader takes steps to correct it, then they may not be charged a penalty.*

*If a trader does not submit their VAT return, then HMRC can issue an assessment showing the amount HMRC believes is due based on their best estimate.*

*Failure to notify HMRC of changes to details of VAT registration such as trading name or address, change of bank account details, change in main business activities or significant changes to types of supply, within 30 days can lead to a penalty.*

## 53 JAHEDA

(a)     The answer is: £0

No late filing penalty is due as this is Jaheda's first late submission, which means she has not reached the 4 points threshold for monthly returns.

**Key answer tips**

Information about this topic is included in the reference material provided in the assessment, so you do not need to learn it.

However, you need to be familiar with its location and content – why not look at it now?

(b)

| | True | False |
|---|---|---|
| Jaheda will potentially receive a penalty point for each of her late submissions. | ✓ | |
| Jaheda will be charged £200 for each of her late submissions. | | ✓ |

Jaheda will most likely receive a penalty point for each of her late submissions but HMRC has the discretion to not to award points if leniency is merited.

Once the threshold is met (4 points in the case of Jaheda as she makes quarterly returns), a £200 penalty is charged.

## 54 LATE PAYMENT

(a) The answer is £100

The first penalty is based on the £5,000 outstanding on day 15 at 2%. The total first penalty will therefore be:

£5,000 x 2% = £100

There are no additional penalties because it was paid within 31 days.

(b) The answer is A.

The first penalty is based on the £3,400 outstanding on day 15 at 2% plus a further 2% of the £3,400 outstanding on day 30. The total first penalty will therefore be:

£3,400 × 4% = £136.

In addition, a second penalty is payable from day 31 onwards at 4% p.a. of the amount still outstanding, calculated on a daily basis

£3,400 × 4% × 45/365 = £16.77

The total penalty payable is therefore £152.77.

If you chose B, you only calculated the first penalty.

If you chose C, you calculated £3,400 × 4% × 75/365.

If you chose D, you only calculated the second penalty.

**Key answer tips**

Information about this topic is included in the reference material provided in the assessment, so you do not need to learn it.

However, you need to be familiar with its location and content – why not look at it now?

## 55 LUCINDA

(a)   The answer is D.

   The error is deliberate but not concealed.

(b)   The answer is C.

   The failure to register is disclosed within 12 months of tax being due. Therefore, a non-deliberate failure can be reduced to 0%.

---

### Tutorial note

*If a business registers late for VAT, VAT is still payable for the period when the business should have been registered. If this cannot be recovered from customers, the supplies made are deemed to include VAT, and this amount must be paid to HMRC.*

*Ignorance of the VAT rules is not a reasonable excuse for failure to register for VAT.*

---

### Key answer tips

Information about this topic is included in the reference material provided in the assessment, so you do not need to learn it.

However, you need to be familiar with its location and content – why not look at it now?

---

## 56 ERRORS AND OMISSIONS

(a)

| Error/omissions | | Action |
|---|---|---|
| Failing to register | C | HMRC can issue an assessment to collect tax due and charge a penalty. |
| Failure to submit a return | B | HMRC can issue an assessment to collect tax due. |
| Making a careless or deliberate error | D | Trader must correct the error and HMRC can charge a penalty. |
| Making a non-careless error | A | Trader must correct the error. |

(b)

| Error/omissions | | Maximum penalty |
|---|---|---|
| Making a deliberate and concealed error | C | 100% of potential lost revenue |
| Submitting a paper VAT return when the online exemption does not apply | F | £400 |
| Failing to notify HMRC within 30 days that the HMRC assessment of VAT is too low | A | 30% of potential lost revenue |

***Tutorial note***

*HMRC can issue a VAT assessment if a VAT return is not submitted in time. This will show an amount of VAT payable. If this is amount is too low, the business will be charged a penalty of 30% if HMRC is not informed within 30 days.*

**Key answer tips**

Information about this topic is included in the reference material provided in the assessment, so you do not need to learn it.

However, you need to be familiar with its location and content – why not look at it now?

# PRINCIPLES OF PAYROLL

## 57    PETRA

(a)    The answer is C.

Rhea has no employees so does not register as an employer. Steve does not operate a business but still employs a nanny so must register. Tamar must register as an employer even if it is her accountants who carry out the payroll procedures.

(b)    The answer is D.

An employer must register before the first payday (28 August in this case) but not more than two months before starting to pay people.

**Key answer tips**

Information about this topic is included in the reference material provided in the assessment, so you do not need to learn it.

However you need to be familiar with its location and content – why not look at it now?

(c)     The answer is C.

HMRC is the relevant tax authority for payroll.

**58     LEYLA**

(a)

|  | True | False |
|---|---|---|
| Failure to keep payroll records gives rise to a penalty of £500. |  | ✓ |
| Employers must submit payroll information online to HMRC using HMRC's software Basic PAYE Tools. |  | ✓ |
| Payroll records must be kept for three years. | ✓ |  |

*Tutorial note*

*Employers with few than ten employees can use HMRC's free software, but are not obliged to do so. Larger employers must use alternative commercial software.*

*The penalty for failure to keep proper payroll records is £3,000. The penalty for failure to keep VAT records is £500.*

**Key answer tips**

Information about this topic is included in the reference material provided in the assessment, so you do not need to learn it.

However, you need to be familiar with its location and content – why not look at it now?

(b)     The answers are A and C.

A business can be picked at random for a PAYE visit, although this may be prompted by errors in an employer's payroll operation.

An error would have to be deliberate and concealed for the maximum penalty to be 100% of potential lost revenue (PLR). The maximum penalty for a deliberate error that is not concealed is 70% of PLR.

**59 MAPPEL LTD**

(a) Mappel Ltd must complete a form <u>P11D</u> to record an employee's benefits for a tax year.

The form must be given to <u>both the employee and HMRC</u>.

The employer must provide the form by <u>6 July</u> following the end of the tax year.

**Key answer tips**

Information about this topic is included in the reference material provided in the assessment, so you do not need to learn it.

However, you need to be familiar with its location and content – why not look at it now?

(b)

| | Principle |
|---|---|
| The payroll department only collects the information needed from an employee to operate payroll correctly. | Data minimisation |
| An employee's bank details are encrypted. | Integrity and security (confidentiality) |
| An instruction on the employees' payslips requests employees check their personal details and inform the payroll department of any changes. | Accuracy |

**60 TOM**

(a)

| | £ |
|---|---|
| Gross pay | 3,000.00 |
| Taxable pay | 2,790.00 |
| Net pay | 2,177.18 |

*Tutorial note*

*The taxable pay is the amount after deductions which receive tax relief i.e. the employee's pension contributions.*

*The net pay is the gross pay after all deductions i.e. the amount actually received by the employee.*

(b)

| | True | False |
|---|---|---|
| The employer must make deductions of PAYE and employee's NIC as these are statutory deductions. | ✓ | |
| The employer must deduct certain pension contributions unless Sanjeev has opted out of auto-enrolment. | ✓ | |
| Sanjeev can opt for his student loan to be repaid directly by deductions from his wages. | | ✓ |
| The restaurant may make deductions for breakages by Sanjeev, provided there is a prior written agreement for this in place. | ✓ | |

**Tutorial note**

*Student loan deductions are not voluntary. They must be made by the employer if applicable.*

**61    JOLENE**

(a)    The answers are A and D.

**Tutorial note**

*A form P45 is issued by an employer to an employee who is leaving the business.   The employee keeps one part of the form and gives the two parts to the new employer.  A copy of the form P45 is only sent to HMRC if the employer is not using the Real Time Information System (RTI).  As most employers must use RTI it is reasonable to assume that would be the case here.*

*The new employer uses the P45 to determine the employee's correct tax code.*

*An employer provides HMRC with details of a new starter on the FPS (Full Payment Submission) when the employee is first paid.*

(b)

| | P60 required | Not required |
|---|---|---|
| Abe – employed throughout the tax year | ✓ | |
| Barbara – left Branch Ltd on 31 January 2024 | | ✓ |
| Careem – joined Branch Ltd on 1 February 2024 | ✓ | |
| David – left Branch Ltd on 30 April 2024. | ✓ | |

An employer must issue a P60 to individuals who were employees at the end of the tax year i.e. here, on 5 April 2025.

## 62   VIKRAM

(a)   The answer is B.

The FPS (Full Payment Submission) must be submitted on or before the date the employees are paid.

(b)

|  | Required | Not required |
|---|---|---|
| Each employee's taxable pay and pay subject to national insurance contributions (NIC) for pay period | ✓ |  |
| Each employee's PAYE and NIC deducted from the October payment | ✓ |  |
| Employer's national insurance contributions for each employee | ✓ |  |
| The leaving date for employees if this is the FPS of their final payment | ✓ |  |
| The starting dates of all employees working in the business |  | ✓ |

*Tutorial note*

*The Full Payment Submission (FPS) gives the pay and deductions information for each employee for the period, and also for the tax year to date on a cumulative basis. Starting dates and leaving dates are given in the first and last FPS for those respective employees.*

*Note that taxable benefits taxed outside of the payroll system are included on form P11D after the end of the year and are not recorded on the FPS during the tax year. An employer can register with HMRC to use the 'payrolling employee's taxable benefits and expenses service' if this is the case then the value of the benefit is included within the FPS.*

**Key answer tips**

Information about this topic is included in the reference material provided in the assessment, so you do not need to learn it.

However, you need to be familiar with its location and content – why not look at it now?

## 63   ANTHONY

(a)   The answer is A.

The Employer Payment Summary (EPS) must be submitted if no payments are made to employees, by 19th of the following month.

(b)

|  | True | False |
|---|---|---|
| The penalty depends on the number of employees of the business | ✓ |  |
| The penalty is charged as a percentage of the deductions showing on the FPS |  | ✓ |
| Karen will avoid a penalty if this is her first late submission in the tax year | ✓ |  |
| If the FPS is submitted within three days of the due date, a penalty is only charged if Karen regularly submits the FPS late. | ✓ |  |
| A further penalty is charged if the FPS is more than six months late |  | ✓ |

Penalties for late filing of FPSs are charged at flat rates, but these increase in steps as the number of employees in the business increases.

The penalties for late payroll payments are different and depend on the number of defaults in the tax year. The penalty is a percentage of the late amount and further penalties are then charged if the payments are more than six or twelve months late.

**Key answer tips**

Information about this topic is included in the reference material provided in the assessment, so you do not need to learn it.

However, you need to be familiar with its location and content – why not look at it now?

(c)   The answer is D.

The information on the P45 relates to the individual's previous employment. The new employer may use the information to set up the individual's details correctly on the payroll system.

# REPORTING INFORMATION ON VAT AND PAYROLL

**Key answer tips**

The chief examiner has said in the past that the most common reason for being not yet competent in questions on this area is not reading the task properly and then failing to provide the correct information to others in the organisation.

For example, where the business's input tax exceeds the output tax for the VAT period there will be a refund due to the business from HMRC, but some candidates failed to appreciate this. They identified the correct value to enter on the e-mail but advised the finance representative to make a payment when a refund is due, or vice versa.

For such a straightforward task, much more care is needed.

## 64 BARCLAY

(a) The answer is D.

Evading VAT is a criminal offence so this is not a good reason to keep up-to-date.

(b) The answers are A and C.

VAT and payroll rules change frequently and often need implementing quickly. Software providers often issue updates on a timely basis to reflect these changes, but an accounting technician working on the VAT return or on payroll must understand these changes. HMRC and GOV.UK are authoritative sources of information whereas social media and a news site are not.

## 65 DHONI LTD

| Email | | |
|---|---|---|
| **To:** | Financial Accountant | |
| **From:** | Accounting technician | |
| **Date:** | 17 January 2025 | |
| **Subject:** | VAT error | |

An error occurred in the VAT return for the previous quarter. Output tax of £4,672.90 was **understated.** This resulted in VAT being **underpaid.**

This error **was included on the VAT return to 31 December 2024.**

Kind regards

*Tutorial note*

*When a trader discovers a VAT error, they must inform HMRC.*

*If the net error is less than a certain threshold and is not deliberate it can be included on the next VAT return. If not, it must be disclosed separately on Form VAT 652 or in a letter.*

*The threshold operates as follows:*

- *Net errors up to £10,000 can always be included on the next VAT return.*
- *Net errors above £50,000 must always be separately disclosed.*

*Errors between these thresholds can be included on the next VAT return if they are no more than 1% of turnover (specifically the figure in Box 6 of the return).*

**Key answer tips**

Information about this topic is included in the reference material provided in the assessment, so you do not need to learn it.

However, you need to be familiar with its location and content – why not look at it now?

66   **BELL**

(a)

| Email | |
|---|---|
| **To:** | Andrew Bell |
| **From:** | Accounting technician |
| **Date:** | 17 April 2025 |
| **Subject:** | Irrecoverable (bad) debt relief |

Thank you for advising me about the debt you wrote off. I have included relief for this in the VAT return for the quarter ended **31 March 2025**.

Relief can be claimed because the debt was due for payment more than **6 months** ago.

The **output** tax paid on the original invoice can be reclaimed by including the amount in **Box 4**. The amount of irrecoverable (bad) debt relief is **£1,077.83**.

Kind regards

(b)

| | Email |
|---|---|
| **To:** | Jessica |
| **From:** | Accounting technician |
| **Date:** | 1 May 2024 |
| **Subject:** | Annual accounting scheme for VAT |

Under the annual accounting scheme you pay **nine** monthly payments of VAT during the accounting period. The first payment is due at the end of **month four** of the accounting period. Each monthly payment is **10%** of the previous year's liability.

A balancing payment is due **two months** after the end of the accounting period.

Kind regards

**Key answer tips**

Information about this topic is included in the reference material provided in the assessment, so you do not need to learn it.

However, you need to be familiar with its location and content – why not look at it now?

## 67   SEABORN LTD

(a)

| | Email |
|---|---|
| **To:** | Financial Accountant |
| **From:** | Accounting Technician |
| **Date:** | 5 September 2024 |
| **Subject:** | Filing VAT returns |

VAT returns must be submitted **quarterly** unless you are a net repayment trader when returns can be made **monthly**.

Returns must be filed within **1 month and 7 days** after the end of the VAT period.

You **must file online.**

Kind regards

**Key answer tips**

Information about this topic is included in the reference material provided in the assessment, so you do not need to learn it.

However, you need to be familiar with its location and content – why not look at it now?

(b)    The answer is D.

It is important to seek authorisation before a VAT return is submitted.

**68    MILES LTD**

| Email |
| --- |
| **To:**        All Sales and Sales Invoicing Staff |
| **From:**     Accounts Assistant |
| **Date:**     14 July 2024 |
| **Subject:**   Change in VAT treatment |
| As you know the company's main product has been reclassified from one that is **zero-rated** to one that is **standard-rated**. |
| All sales invoices **with a tax point on or after 1 September** must have the standard rate of VAT applied. |
| As we have decided to keep our VAT-inclusive prices the same, the price of goods to our customers will **stay the same** and our profits will **decrease**. |
| Kind regards |

**69    ELSIE**

(a)    The answer is C.

It is important that you identify when a query about VAT is beyond your current expertise and hence refer it to a line manager.

(b)    The answer is D.

Information in a VAT return is confidential.

**70    JEFF**

(a)    The answer is payable to HMRC is £1,756.84 (£621.50 + £462.96 + £557.52 + £114.86).

The payment to HMRC includes PAYE, employee's and employer's national insurance contributions, and student loan deductions. The pension contributions are not paid to HMRC but are invested in the pension fund.

(b)    The answer is 22 September 2024.

(c)    If this is the first late payment for the tax year, there is no penalty.

If this is not the first late payment for the tax year, the penalty depends on the number of late payments in the tax year.

**71   OLGA**

   (a)   The answers are A and B.

       Olga must keep up-to-date with changes to payroll law and should prepare the P11Ds using the relevant law for that tax year.

       She should run software updates on a timely basis as instructed by the software provider. Deliberately including incorrect information on the P11Ds to pay less tax will lead to penalties. It is against ethical principles and is tax evasion.

       Olga should seek authorisation before submitting the P11Ds and if she is uncertain about how to complete them, she should ask her manager.

   (b)   The answers are C and D.

       HMRC has powers to visit business premises and inspect payroll records.

       Data must not be kept for longer than the purpose required, but the law requires payroll records must be kept for three years.

# Section 3

# MOCK ASSESSMENT QUESTIONS

## ASSESSMENT INFORMATION

You have **1 hour 30 minutes** to complete this mock assessment.

- This assessment contains **8 tasks** and you should attempt to complete **every** task,

- Each task is independent. You will not need to refer to your answers to previous tasks.

- The total number of marks for this assessment is **80**.

- Read every task carefully to make sure you understand what is required.

- Where the date is relevant, it is given in the task data.

- Both minus signs and brackets can be used to indicate negative numbers **unless** task instructions state otherwise.

- You must us a full stop to indicate a decimal point. For example, write 100.57 **not** 100,57 or 10057.

- You may use a comma to indicate a number in the thousands, but you don't have to. For example, 10000 and 10,000 are both acceptable.

- If your answer requires rounding, apply normal mathematical rules **unless** the task instructions say otherwise.

## TASK 1 (9 marks)

This task is about understanding and calculating UK tax law principles relating to VAT, registration and deregistration and special schemes.

This task contains parts (a) to (d).

Joe starts his business on 1 June 2024.

He has taxable supplies of £9,100 per month.

**(a)** **Complete the following statements.** **(3 marks)**

(i) Joe needs to notify HMRC by Day _____Month_____Year_____

(ii) Joe will be registered from Day _____Month_____Year_____

**Options**

| Day | Month | Year |
|-----|-------|------|
| 1 | March | 2024 |
| 7 | April | 2025 |
| 30 | May | |
| 31 | June | |

---

(iii)    Joe......... register voluntarily before this date.

**Options**
can
cannot

**(b)    Identify whether the following statements are true or false.  (3 marks)**

Tick the correct box for each statement.

|  | True ✓ | False ✓ |
|---|---|---|
| A business has an expected turnover for the next 12 months of £92,000 but it sells goods that are zero-rated so it cannot register for VAT. |  |  |
| Exempt supplies are not chargeable to VAT. |  |  |
| A business using the flat rate scheme applies the flat rate percentage to its VAT-exclusive turnover. |  |  |

**(c)    Identify which of the following is an advantage of the annual accounting scheme. (1 mark)**

A    It is good for businesses that are experiencing a decrease in turnover compared to previous years.

B    It is beneficial for businesses that have a repayment due to them rather than having to make a payment of VAT.

C    It reduces the amount of administration work to be completed.

D    It provides automatic bad debt relief.

Jasper Enterprises uses the annual accounting scheme. Their annual period ends on 31 May. The VAT liability for the year ended 31 May 2023 is £6,980 and for the year ended 31 May 2024 is £7,211.

**(d)    Calculate the amount of the payments for Jasper Enterprises for the year ended 31 May 2024.                                                                                      (2 marks)**

(i)    Each monthly payment on account for Jasper Enterprises for the year ended 31 May 2024 should be

    [                    ]

(ii)    The balancing payment for Jasper Enterprises for the year ended 31 May 2024 is

    [                    ]

**TASK 2  (8 marks)**

This task is about calculating and accounting for VAT.

This task contains parts (a) to (d).

Beetroot Ltd makes a purchase of materials on sale or return. The goods are delivered on 12 May 2024 and must be accepted or returned by 31 August 2024. The business decides to accept the goods on 20 July 2024 and pays for them on 30 July 2024. The invoice was issued on 10 August 2024.

**(a)   Identify the actual tax point for this purchase.**                                      **(1 mark)**

A     12 May 2024

B     20 July 2024

C     30 July 2024

D     10 August 2024

You send a sales credit note to a customer for £40 plus VAT at the standard rate.

**(b)   Identify the effect that this has on the amount of VAT payable to HMRC by your business.**
                                                                                                                **(1 mark)**

A     The amount payable will decrease by £40

B     The amount payable will increase by £40

C     The amount payable will decrease by £8

D     The amount payable will increase by £8

**(c)   Identify whether the following items need to be included or not included on a full VAT invoice.**                                                                                 **(4 marks)**

|  | Include ✓ | Do not include ✓ |
|---|---|---|
| Identifying number |  |  |
| Delivery date |  |  |
| Total amount of VAT payable |  |  |
| Customer's registration number |  |  |

Martine has asked you to show her how to calculate VAT at the reduced rate on net amounts.

**(d)   Complete the following table to assist Martine. Round down your answers to the nearest penny.**                                                                                 **(2 marks)**

| Net £ | VAT £ | Gross £ |
|---|---|---|
| 272.13 |  |  |

**TASK 3** **(12 marks)**

This task is about the recovery of input tax.

This task contains parts (a) to (e).

Wolf Ltd supplies goods that are a mixture of standard-rated and exempt.

**(a)** **Identify which one of the following statements is true in relation to Wolf Ltd.** **(1 mark)**

A All of the input VAT can be reclaimed.

B None of the input VAT can be reclaimed.

C All of the input VAT can be reclaimed provided certain de minimis conditions are met.

D Only the input VAT on goods and services purchased for use in making standard-rated supplies can ever be reclaimed.

Low Ltd is a VAT registered business making taxable supplies only. The company has incurred the expenditure shown below in the last month. All purchases were for business purposes other than the car, which is used by the managing director for both business and private mileage.

**(b)** **Identify whether input VAT can be reclaimed on each item of expenditure.** **(4 marks)**

| Item | Net £ | VAT £ | Gross £ | Reclaim? ✓ |
|---|---|---|---|---|
| Motor car | 2,500.00 | 500.00 | 3,000.00 | |
| Stationery | 25.00 | 5.00 | 30.00 | |
| Fixtures and fittings | 1,212.00 | 242.40 | 1,454.40 | |
| Staff entertaining | 250.00 | 50.00 | 300.00 | |

You have been given the following information about the business transactions of Illusion Ltd for the quarter ended 31 December 2024.

|  | £ |
|---|---|
| Sales of standard-rated items | 250,000 |
| Sales of zero-rated items | 100,000 |
| Purchases of goods relating to standard-rated supplies | 162,000 |
| Purchases of goods relating to zero-rated supplies | 21,500 |

**(c)** **Complete the following statement in relation to Illusion Ltd.** **(1 mark)**

Illusion Ltd can reclaim input tax on ................................................................

**Options**

purchases of goods relating to standard-rated supplies only

purchases of all goods subject to certain de minimis conditions

all purchases

The credit controller of Fulfilled Ltd has carried out a review of aged receivables at the end of the financial year to 31 December and written off some irrecoverable debts.

Fulfilled Ltd does not operate any special VAT schemes. All supplies are standard-rated.

**(d)** For each irrecoverable debt written off:

**(i)** Identify whether the debt is or is not eligible for bad debt relief. **(2 marks)**

**(ii)** Calculate the amount of bad debt relief available. Round down figures to the nearest penny. **(2 marks)**

| Bad debt | Eligible for bad debt relief ✓ | Not eligible for bad debt relief ✓ | Amount of bad debt relief available £ |
|---|---|---|---|
| Motion Ltd has an eight-month old irrecoverable debt on a sales invoice for £1,250 including VAT | | | |
| Stationary Ltd has a five-month old irrecoverable debt on a sales invoice for £1,212 excluding VAT. | | | |

Leaf Ltd received an invoice from a supplier totalling £2,000.00 excluding VAT at the standard rate. The supplier offered Leaf Ltd a 5% prompt payment discount if payment was received within ten days. Leaf Ltd took advantage of the prompt payment discount.

**(e)** Calculate the amount that Leaf Ltd can recover as input tax. Round down to the nearest penny. **(2 marks)**

Leaf Ltd can reclaim input tax of £............................................

**TASK 4 (8 marks)**

This task is about preparing, calculating and adjusting information for VAT returns.

Yasmin is an accounting technician who works for a firm of accountants. She is working on the VAT return for Loft Ltd for the quarter ended 30 June 2024 using a software package that is compatible with making tax digital. Loft Ltd is a VAT registered business making taxable supplies only.

Yasmin would like to know the impact of raising a credit note in respect of an invoice to one of Loft Ltd's customers, Ball Ltd. The original invoice was for £750 net of VAT, Loft Ltd did not account for any discounts when the original invoice was raised. Ball Ltd subsequently took advantage of the 8% prompt payment discount. Loft Ltd will raise a credit note in respect of the prompt payment discount taken.

**(a)** **(i)** Calculate the reduction to the output VAT as a result of raising the credit note. Round down to the nearest penny. **(1 mark)**

| Reduction in output tax £ |
|---|
| |

Loft Ltd trades internationally. Yasmin has asked you for some help with postponed accounting for VAT.

**Complete the following statements to help Yasmin with postponed accounting.   (2 marks)**

**(ii)**   Postponed accounting relates only to purchases of ...................................................

**Options**

goods

services

**(iii)**   Postponed accounting relates only to purchases from ...................................... suppliers.

**Options**

UK

overseas

Yasmin has identified three transactions that need to be posted in the accounting software.

**(iv)**   **Calculate the adjustments to be made to the figures for output tax and input tax for each transaction. Round down your answers to the nearest penny. If no adjustment is required, enter 0.00.**                                  **(3 marks)**

| Date | Transaction | Output tax £ | Input tax £ |
|---|---|---|---|
| 8 May 2024 | Overtime payment of £500 to an employee. | | |
| 9 May 2024 | Cash proceeds of £678.90 from the sale of machinery. Loft Ltd had reclaimed the VAT on the original purchase. | | |
| 10 May 2024 | VAT paid to HMRC for the quarter ended 31 March 2024 of £1,212.35 | | |

Yasmin has entered a payment, into the accounting software, to Loft Ltd's electricity supplier totalling £131.25 including VAT at the reduced rate. The accounting software has calculated the VAT as £6.25 but the invoice shows VAT as £21.88.

**(v)**   **Identify the correct action to be taken by Yasmin.**                            **(2 marks)**

| Action | Select the correct action ✓ |
|---|---|
| Yasmin should make no adjustment and use the figure generated by the software. | |
| Yasmin should make an adjustment and use the figure shown on the invoice. | |
| Yasmin should check which rate of VAT is correct and query with the supplier whether the reduced rate applies. | |

**TASK 5  (12 marks)**

This task is about verifying VAT returns.

This task contains parts (a) to (b).

(a)  **For each of the following businesses, identify whether they can correct the (non-deliberate) errors on their next VAT return or whether they are required to make separate disclosure.**

**(3 marks)**

|  | On next return ✓ | Separate disclosure ✓ |
|---|---|---|
| (i)   A business with a net error of £15,552 and a turnover of £2,800,000. | | |
| (ii)  A business with a net error of £8,032 and a turnover of £58,000. | | |
| (iii) A business with a net error of £12,156 and a turnover of £810,000. | | |

Thimble Ltd uses accounting software to calculate the VAT due to or from HMRC. Thimble has recently joined the cash accounting scheme, this is the first quarter of reporting under the scheme.

Francesca, an accounting technician, has completed the draft VAT return for the quarter ended 30 September 2024. The finance director has asked her to complete a reconciliation to the trial balance to confirm the accuracy of the figures before the return is submitted.

The draft VAT return contains the following figures:

| Box | £ |
|---|---|
| 1 | 34,600.00 |
| 4 | (15,570.00) |
| 5 | 19,030.00 |

The VAT liability in the trial balance shows a liability of £16,050. Francesca has also obtained the following information for the quarter to 30 September 2024.

|  | £ |
|---|---|
| Payments to suppliers (inclusive of standard-rated VAT) | 84,900 |
| Receipts from customers (inclusive of standard-rated VAT) | 181,200 |

(b)  (i)  **Identify whether the following statements are true or false.**  **(3 marks)**

|  | True ✓ | False ✓ |
|---|---|---|
| A possible reason for the difference between the VAT due in the draft VAT return and the figure on the trial balance is that the software used to complete the return has accidentally not been set up for cash accounting. | | |
| Francesca should correct the VAT return next quarter to take account of the differences she has found. | | |
| VAT on payables is known as output VAT. | | |

(ii) Complete the table below to reconcile the figure in the draft VAT return to the figure in the trial balance. Use minus signs to indicate negative figures where appropriate.

(4 marks)

|  | £ |
|---|---|
| Amount due per draft VAT return |  |
| VAT on receivables |  |
| VAT on payables |  |
| VAT liability per the trial balance | 16,050.00 |

(iii) For each of the following overseas supplies, identify whether an entry is required in Box 1 or Box 6 of the VAT return, tick all boxes that apply. (2 marks)

|  | Box 1 | Box 6 |
|---|---|---|
|  | ✓ | ✓ |
| Exports of goods |  |  |
| Supply of services to overseas business customers |  |  |

## TASK 6 (11 marks)

This task is about VAT rules on record keeping, filing and payment/repayment, including non-compliance implications.

This task contains parts (a) to (d).

You work for a company that pays its VAT by direct debit.

The accountant asks you when the company's VAT payment of £1,900 for the quarter ended 31 March 2024 will be taken from the company bank account.

Today's date is Wednesday 24 April 2024.

Assume that the bank working days are Monday to Friday only and that there is a Bank Holiday on Friday 10 May 2024.

(a) (i) Identify the date on which the direct debit will be taken from the company bank account. (1 mark)

A    Tuesday 30 April

B    Friday 10 May

C    Monday 13 May

D    Tuesday 14 May

The accountant advises he was 45 days late making the company's VAT payment of £1,900 for the quarter ended 31 March 2024.

(ii) Calculate the amount of the first late payment penalty in relation to this quarter. Enter the amount to two decimal places. (1 mark)

(iii) Calculate the amount of the second late payment penalty in relation to this quarter. Enter the amount to two decimal places. (1 mark)

**(b)** **Identify whether the following statements are true or false.** **(6 marks)**

Tick the correct box for each statement.

| | True ✓ | False ✓ |
|---|---|---|
| VAT records should normally be kept for 4 years. | | |
| The penalty for failure to keep VAT records is £500. | | |
| If a business fails to register for VAT then HMRC will collect any VAT due but will not issue a penalty. | | |
| A business has prepared its VAT return for the quarter ended 31 March 2024; it must pay by electronic transfer by 30 April 2024. | | |
| A business that always submits its VAT on time, but for the first time submits its VAT return late, will be issued with a late filing penalty point and £200 penalty charge. | | |
| If a business makes a careless error, it must notify HMRC and may be charged a penalty. | | |

Crystal Ltd operates the annual accounting scheme and output tax always exceeds input tax. The VAT period ends on 30 June and Crystal Ltd makes quarterly VAT payments.

**(c)** **Identify the correct payment information by completing the following statements.**

**(2 marks)**

Crystal Ltd must make ..................................... payments in any calendar year.

**Options**

three

four

The due date of the VAT return for Crystal Ltd is .....................................

**Options**

31 July

31 August

**TASK 7 (12 marks)**

This task is about principles of payroll.

This task contains parts (a) to (c).

**(a)** **Identify whether the following statements relate to a full payment submission (FPS) or an employer payment summary (EPS). (4 marks)**

|  | FPS ✓ | EPS ✓ |
|---|---|---|
| Filed by an employer if no employees were paid in the tax month. |  |  |
| Includes the National Insurance number of employees paid in the period. |  |  |
| Includes the postcode of employees paid in the period. |  |  |
| Sent to HMRC by the 19th of the following tax month. |  |  |

Gold Ltd has a total monthly payroll bill in excess of £1,500 and pays the amount of income tax, national insurance and other deductions due to HMRC electronically. The company accountant is concerned that some payroll deadlines have been missed.

**(b)** **Identify whether the following payroll activities were completed on time or late. (3 marks)**

| Date | Payroll activity | On time ✓ | Late ✓ |
|---|---|---|---|
| 25 May 2024 | Paid HMRC in relation to salaries paid on the last Friday in April 2024. |  |  |
| 29 May 2024 | Distributed the P60s for 2023/24 to staff. |  |  |
| 15 July 2024 | Submitted expenses and benefits forms to HMRC in relation to 2023/24. |  |  |

Mia has asked you for some help with understanding her tax code and P60.

**(c)** **(i)** **Complete the following statement to explain the purpose of tax codes.** **(1 mark)**

An employee's tax code is used by an employer to calculate the amount of ............................................. that is due to HMRC for the employee .

**Options**

income tax

national insurance contributions (NIC)

Mia has been in employment for 10 months, her annual salary is £85,680. Mia's P60 shows tax deducted of £15,992.00 and employee's national insurance contributions of £5,306.84.

(ii) **Complete the table below to show the amounts received by Mia in 2023/24. Enter all amounts to two decimal places. Use a minus sign to show any deductions from pay.** **(3 marks)**

| | £ |
|---|---|
| Gross pay per P60 | |
| PAYE | |
| Employee's national insurance contributions | |
| Net pay amount per P60 in 2023/24 | |

Mia is considering giving to charity through her employer's give as you earn scheme.

(iii) **Complete the following statement about give as you earn schemes.** **(1 mark)**

An employer deducts give as you earn contributions........................calculation of income tax on the employee's earnings.

**Options**
before
after

## TASK 8 (8 marks)

This task is about reporting information on VAT and payroll.

This task contains part (a) and (b).

You are an accounting technician working as Accounts Assistant for Wags Dog Walkers Ltd. Within the company responsibility for payroll matters is divided up as follows:

- You prepare the monthly payroll.

- The supervisor of the dog walkers approves all hours worked by those staff members.

- All payments are approved and paid by the managing director, one of two 50% shareholders in the company.

- The year-end financial statements are prepared by the finance director, the other 50% shareholder in the company.

- The supervisor of the dog walkers has informed you that one of the staff members will be going on maternity leave later in the year. The supervisor believes that the staff member will be entitled to statutory maternity pay.

You have prepared the wages report for March 2025, but this hasn't been approved yet.

(a)   (i)   **Complete the email to the correct person, regarding the wages report.**   **(4 marks)**

| To: | Option 1 |
|---|---|
| **From:** | Accounting Technician |
| **Date:** | 7 April 2025 |
| **RE:** | Wages report for approval |

Please find attached the wages report for quarter end 31 March 2025.

Can I ask that you take a look and if you are happy with the contents, please reply to this email to approve it.

May I draw your attention to the detail of statutory maternity pay. I have researched this using two methods | Option 2 | and | Option 3 |

Once you are happy with the report and you have approved it, I will send it to

| Option 4 | to ensure the numbers contained within the report are

included in the year end accounts.

Please do not hesitate to contact me with any questions, otherwise I look forward to hearing from you.

Kind Regards

Accounting Technician.

**Option 1**
the supervisor of the dog walkers
the managing director
the finance director

**Option 2**
The gov.uk website.
my cousin, who recently had a baby.
the finance director.
mummies.com, a popular web forum for new mothers.

**Option 3**
The gov.uk website.
my cousin, who recently had a baby.
the finance director.
mummies.com, a popular web forum for new mothers.

**Options 4**

the supervisor of the dog walkers

the managing director

the finance director

(ii) **The payments to the staff and HMRC will be made by** (1 mark)

**Options**

the supervisor of the dog walkers

the managing director

the finance director

(b) **Identify whether the following statements are true or false?** (3 marks)

|  | True ✓ | False ✓ |
|---|---|---|
| Payroll records must be retained for six years from the end of the tax year to which they relate. |  |  |
| The penalty for failure the retain payroll records is based on the number of employees in the relevant tax year. |  |  |
| The penalty for a late payroll payment is based on the number of defaults that the business has already made in the tax year. |  |  |

# Section 4

# MOCK ASSESSMENT ANSWERS

**TASK 1**

(a) (i) 30 April 2025

The trader exceeds the registration threshold after 10 months' trading – by the end of March 2025. He must notify HMRC by 30 days after the end of the month in which he exceeded the threshold.

(ii) 1 May 2025.

VAT registration is effective by the first day of the second month after the month the threshold is exceeded.

(iii) Joe **can** register voluntarily before this date – Any business that makes some taxable supplies can register voluntarily.

**Key answer tips**

Information about this topic is included in the reference material provided in the real assessment, so you do not need to learn it.

However, you need to be familiar with its location and content – why not look at it now?

(b)

|  | True ✓ | False ✓ |
|---|---|---|
| A business has an expected turnover for the next 12 months of £92,000 but it sells goods that are zero-rated so it cannot register for VAT. |  | ✓ |
| Exempt supplies are not chargeable to VAT. | ✓ |  |
| A business using the flat rate scheme applies the flat rate percentage to its VAT-exclusive turnover. |  | ✓ |

*Tutorial note*

*Traders who make zero-rated supplies are making taxable supplies and **can** register for VAT.*

*A business using the flat rate scheme calculates its liability by multiplying the flat rate percentage by the VAT-inclusive turnover.*

(c)    (i)    The answer is C

**Tutorial note**

*The annual accounting scheme is not useful for businesses that are experiencing lower turnover than the previous year as the payments on account are based on the previous year's turnover not the current year.*

*For repayment businesses, they would have to wait longer for their refund if they are only completing one return per annum.*

*The cash accounting scheme provides automatic bad debt relief, not the annual accounting scheme.*

(ii)    The answer is £698 (£6,980 × 10%).

The POAs are always based on the previous year's VAT liability.

(iii)    The answer is £929.

The POAs are paid at the end of months 4 to 12 so there are nine instalments.

(9 months × £698) = £6,282 paid during the year.

This year's liability is £7,211 so the difference is the balancing payment

i.e. (£7,211 – £6,282) = £929

## TASK 2

(a)    The answer is B

**Tutorial note**

*The basic tax point is the date by which the goods must be accepted provided that is less than 12 months after the date the goods were sent.*

*However, if the goods are accepted before this date, then the date of acceptance becomes the actual tax point.*

(b)    The answer is C

The amount payable will decrease by £8. The VAT on the credit note is £8 (£40 × 20%) and this will reduce the amount the business needs to pay HMRC. This has the same effect as VAT on a purchase.

(c)

|  | Include ✓ | Do not include ✓ |
|---|---|---|
| Identifying number | ✓ |  |
| Delivery date |  | ✓ |
| Total amount of VAT payable | ✓ |  |
| Customer's registration number |  | ✓ |

**Key answer tips**

Information about this topic is included in the reference material provided in the real assessment, so you do not need to learn it.

However, you need to be familiar with its location and content – why not look at it now?

(d)

| Net £ | VAT £ | Gross £ |
|---|---|---|
| 272.13 | 13.60 | 285.73 |

*Tutorial note*

*The VAT is calculated at the reduced rate of 5% (£272.13 × 5%). The gross figure is calculated by adding the net (VAT-exclusive) amount to the VAT to get the VAT-inclusive amount.*

## TASK 3

(a)    The answer is C

A partially exempt trader can reclaim all input tax as long as the de minimis tests are met. If failed only the input tax relating to taxable supplies can be reclaimed.

(b)

| Item | Net £ | VAT £ | Gross £ | Reclaim? |
|---|---|---|---|---|
| Motor car | 2,500.00 | 500.00 | 3,000.00 |  |
| Stationery | 25.00 | 5.00 | 30.00 | ✓ |
| Fixtures and fittings | 1,212.00 | 242.40 | 1,454.40 | ✓ |
| Staff entertaining | 250.00 | 50.00 | 300.00 | ✓ |

**Tutorial note**

*Since the car is used for both business and private mileage the input VAT on its purchase cannot be reclaimed.*

**Key answer tips**

Information about this topic is included in the reference material provided in the real assessment, so you do not need to learn it.

However, you need to be familiar with its location and content – why not look at it now?

(c)     The answer is all purchases.

**Tutorial note**

*Do not confuse exempt supplies with zero-rated supplies. Illusion only makes taxable supplies and so all input VAT can be recovered unless it is a 'blocked' item.*

(d)

| Bad debt | Eligible for bad debt relief ✓ | Not eligible for bad debt relief ✓ | Amount of bad debt relief available £ |
|---|---|---|---|
| Motion Ltd has an eight-month old irrecoverable debt on a sales invoice for £1,250 including VAT | ✓ | | 208.33 |
| Stationary Ltd has a five-month old irrecoverable debt on a sales invoice for £1,212 excluding VAT. | | ✓ | 0.00 |

**Tutorial note**

*Bad debt relief is available on the debt of Motion Ltd as it is over six months old. The relief available is calculated as £1,250 × 1/6.*

(e)    £380.00 (£2,000 × 95% × 20%)

**Tutorial note**

*For a supply of goods, VAT is always calculated on the amount that the customer finally pays.*

**TASK 4**

(a)    (i)    £12.00

The original invoice will have included VAT of £150.00 (£750.00 × 20%). After the discount, the VAT payable is £138.00 (£750 × 92% × 20%).  This is a reduction of £12.00.

(ii)    Postponed accounting relates only to purchases of **goods**.

(iii)   Postponed accounting relates only to purchases from **overseas** suppliers.

**Tutorial note**

*Services supplied to UK businesses from an overseas supplier are accounted for using the reverse charge procedure not postponed accounting.*

(iv)

| Date | Transaction | Output tax £ | Input tax £ |
|------|-------------|-------------|------------|
| 8 May 2024 | Overtime payment of £500 to an employee. | 0.00 | 0.00 |
| 9 May 2024 | Cash proceeds of £678.90 from the sale of machinery. Loft Ltd had reclaimed the VAT on the original purchase. | 113.15 | 0.00 |
| 10 May 2024 | VAT paid to HMRC for the quarter ended 31 March 2024 of £1,212.35 | 0.00 | 0.00 |

**Tutorial note**

*Wages and salaries are outside the scope of VAT so do not appear on the VAT return.*

*If you are asked to show your answers in a certain way (for example showing pounds and pence) it is important to ensure you do so. For those transactions with no impact on the VAT return in this question you needed to include 0.00, not leave the box blank.*

(v)

| Action | Select the correct action ✓ |
|---|---|
| Yasmin should make no adjustment and use the figure generated by the software. | |
| Yasmin should make an adjustment and use the figure shown on the invoice. | |
| Yasmin should check which rate of VAT is correct and query with the supplier whether the reduced rate applies. | ✓ |

## TASK 5

(a)

| | | On next return ✓ | Separate disclosure ✓ |
|---|---|---|---|
| (i) | A business with a net error of £15,552 and a turnover of £2,800,000. | ✓ | |
| (ii) | A business with a net error of £8,032 and a turnover of £58,000. | ✓ | |
| (iii) | A business with a net error of £12,156 and a turnover of £810,000. | | ✓ |

*Tutorial note*

*When a trader discovers a VAT error, they must inform HMRC. If the net error is less than a certain threshold and is not deliberate, it can be included on the next VAT return. If not, it must be disclosed separately on Form VAT 652 or in a letter.*

*The threshold operates as follows:*

*Net errors up to £10,000 can always be included on the next VAT return.*

*Net errors above £50,000 must always be separately disclosed.*

*Errors between these thresholds can be included on the next VAT return if they are no more than 1% of turnover (specifically the figure in Box 6 of the return).*

(b)    (i)

|  | True | False |
|---|---|---|
|  | ✓ | ✓ |
| A possible reason for the difference between the VAT due in the draft VAT return and the figure on the trial balance is that the software used to complete the return has accidentally not been set up for cash accounting. | ✓ |  |
| Francesca should correct the VAT return next quarter to take account of the differences she has found. |  | ✓ |
| VAT on payables is known as output VAT. |  | ✓ |

*Tutorial note*

*Francesca, or a colleague, should arrange for the software to be set up correctly and review the revised return once this has been done.*

*VAT on payables is known as input VAT.*

(ii)

|  | £ |
|---|---|
| Amount due per draft VAT return | 19,030.00 |
| Vat on receivables | –4,400.00 |
| VAT on payables | 1,420.00 |
| VAT liability per the trial balance | 16,050.00 |

| Cash basis | Gross £ | VAT £ | Working £ |
|---|---|---|---|
| Received from customers | 181,200 | 30,200 | 181,200 × 1/6 |
| Paid to suppliers | 84,900 | 14,150 | 84,900 × 1/6 |
| Net Vat due |  | 16,050 |  |
| **Accruals/standard basis** |  |  |  |
| Sales |  | 34,600 |  |
| Purchases |  | 15,570 |  |
| Net VAT due |  | 19,030 |  |

Reduction in output tax due to cash not yet received from customers = £34,600 – £30,200 = £4,400

Increase in input tax due to cash payments not yet made to suppliers = £15,570 – £14,150 = £1,420

**Tutorial note**

*The amount due according to the draft VAT return is the figure from Box 5.*

(iii)

| | Box 1 | Box 6 |
|---|---|---|
| | ✓ | ✓ |
| Exports of goods | | ✓ |
| Supply of services to overseas business customers | | ✓ |

## TASK 6

(a) (i) The answer is C

The normal payment date is seven days after 30 April i.e. 7 May.

Payments by direct debit are taken from the business bank account three working days after the normal payment date. Three working days after Tuesday 7 May will be Monday May 13. (Saturdays, Sundays and Bank Holidays are not working days so are excluded.)

(ii) The answer is: £76.00

The first penalty is based on the £1,900 outstanding on day 15 at 2% plus a further 2% of the £1,900 outstanding on day 30. The total first penalty will therefore be:

£1,900 × 4% = £76.00

(iii) The answer is: £3.12

The second penalty is payable from day 31 onwards at 4% p.a. of the amount still outstanding, calculated on a daily basis

£1,900 × 4% × 15/365 = £3.12

**Key answer tips**

Information about this topic is included in the reference material provided in the real assessment, so you do not need to learn it.

However, you need to be familiar with its location and content – why not look at it now?

In the real assessment this question is likely to be tested through a question using a date picker from a calendar.

(b)

| | True ✓ | False ✓ |
|---|---|---|
| VAT records should normally be kept for 4 years. | | ✓ |
| The penalty for failure to keep VAT records is £500. | ✓ | |
| If a business fails to register for VAT, then HMRC will collect any VAT due but will not issue a penalty. | | ✓ |
| A business has prepared its VAT return for the quarter ended 31 March 2024; it must pay by electronic transfer by 30 April 2024. | | ✓ |
| A business that always submits its VAT on time, but for the first time submits its VAT return late, will be issued with a late filing penalty point and £200 penalty charge. | | ✓ |
| If a business makes a careless error, it must notify HMRC and may be charged a penalty. | ✓ | |

**Tutorial note**

*VAT records should be kept for six years. If a business fails to keep adequate VAT records, then a penalty of £500 can apply.*

*If a business fails to register for VAT, it may be issued with a penalty.*

*The deadline for paying VAT is one months and seven days after the end of the VAT period, but if payment is made by direct debit HMRC will collect 3 **working** days after the submission deadline.*

*When a business submits its VAT return late, it may receive a penalty. The first time that this happens a business may receive a penalty point. The business will only receive a penalty charge of £200 after the points received exceed a set threshold. The threshold of points is dependent on the submission frequency of the VAT return.*

*All errors must be notified to HMRC in the approved manner. Careless or deliberate errors may suffer a penalty.*

**Key answer tips**

Information about this topic is included in the reference material provided in the real assessment, so you do not need to learn it.

However, you need to be familiar with its location and content – why not look at it now?

(c)     Crystal Ltd must make **four** payments in any calendar year.

The due date of the VAT return for Crystal Ltd is **31 August.**

*Tutorial note*

*Crystal Ltd must make three interim payments (25% of the estimated VAT bill based on previous returns) at the end of months 4, 7 and 10 in the accounting period (31 October, 31 January, 30 April) and a balancing payment 2 months after the end of the accounting period (31 August). The due date for the VAT return is the same day as the due date for the balancing payment.*

**Key answer tips**

Information about this topic is included in the reference material provided in the real assessment, so you do not need to learn it.

However, you need to be familiar with its location and content – why not look at it now?

**TASK 7**

(a)

|  | FPS ✓ | EPS ✓ |
|---|---|---|
| Filed by an employer if no employees were paid in the tax month. |  | ✓ |
| Includes the National Insurance number of employees paid in the period. | ✓ |  |
| Includes the postcode of employees paid in the period. | ✓ |  |
| Sent to HMRC by the 19th of the following tax month. |  | ✓ |

**Key answer tips**

Information about this topic is included in the reference material provided in the real assessment, so you do not need to learn it.

However, you need to be familiar with its location and content – why not look at it now?

(b)

| Date | Payroll activity | On time ✓ | Late ✓ |
|------|------------------|-----------|--------|
| 25 May 2024 | Paid HMRC in relation to salaries paid on the last Friday in April 2024. | | ✓ |
| 29 May 2024 | Distributed the P60s for 2023/24 to staff. | ✓ | |
| 15 July 2024 | Submitted expenses and benefits forms to HMRC in relation to 2023/24. | | ✓ |

*Tutorial note*

*The payment date for monthly payroll is 22nd of each month if paid electronically or 19th otherwise.*

*P60s for 2023/24 to must be distributed to staff by 31 May 2024.*

*The filing deadline for expenses and benefits forms in relation to 2023/24 is 6 July 2024.*

**Key answer tips**

Information about this topic is included in the reference material provided in the real assessment, so you do not need to learn it.

However, you need to be familiar with its location and content – why not look at it now?

(c)   (i)   The correct answer is: income tax.

(ii)

| | £ |
|---|---|
| Gross pay per P60 | 71,400.00 |
| PAYE | −15,992.00 |
| Employee's national insurance contributions | −5,306.84 |
| Net pay amount per P60 in 2023/24 | 50,101.16 |

Gross pay is calculated for the time in employment as £85,680 × 10/12.

(iii)   The correct answer is: before.

**TASK 8**

| To: | the managing director |
|---|---|
| From: | Accounting Technician |
| Date: | 7 April 2025 |
| RE: | Wages report for approval |

Please find attached the wages report for quarter end 31 March 2025.

Can I ask that you take a look and if you are happy with the contents, please reply to this email to approve it.

May I draw your attention to the detail of statutory maternity pay. I have researched this using two methods [ The gov.uk website ] and [ the finance director ]

Once you are happy with the report and you have approved it, I will send it to

[ the finance director ] to ensure the numbers contained within the report are

included in the year end accounts.

Please do not hesitate to contact me with any questions, otherwise I look forward to hearing from you.


Kind Regards

Accounting Technician.

(a)  (ii)  The payments to the staff and HMRC will be made by **the managing director**.

(b)

| | True ✓ | False ✓ |
|---|---|---|
| Payroll records must be retained for six years from the end of the tax year to which they relate. | | ✓ |
| The penalty for failure the retain payroll records is based on the number of employees in the relevant tax year. | | ✓ |
| The penalty for a late payroll payment is based on the number of defaults that the business has already made in the tax year. | ✓ | |

*Tutorial note*

*Payroll records must be retained for three years from the end of the tax year to which they relate.*

*The penalty for failure the retain payroll records is a fixed amount of £3,000. The penalty for late submission of payroll filings is based on the number of employees in the relevant tax year.*

**Key answer tips**

Information about this topic is included in the reference material provided in the real assessment, so you do not need to learn it.

However, you need to be familiar with its location and content – why not look at it now?